ARIEL

The Life of Shelley

ANDRÉ MAUROIS

ARIEL

The Life of Shelley

FREDERICK UNGAR PUBLISHING CO.
NEW YORK

CARL A. RUDISILL LIBRARY
LENOIR RHYNE COLLEGE

Translated by Ella D'Arcy

Copyright 1924 by D. Appleton and Company

Copyright renewed 1952 by John Lane,
The Bodley Head, Ltd.

Republished by arrangement
with Appleton-Century-Crofts, Inc.

821.7
M44a

8 98 11
Sept 1974

Sixth Printing, 1972

Printed in the United States of America
ISBN 0-8044-6483-9
Library of Congress Catalog Card Number 57-12326

CONTENTS

PART I

CONTENTS

PART II

FIRST PART

So I turned to the Garden of Love
That so many sweet flowers bore;
And I saw it was filled with graves.

WILLIAM BLAKE.

ARIEL

CHAPTER I

KEATE'S WAY

IN the year 1809 George III appointed as Headmaster of Eton, Dr. Keate, a terrible little man who considered the flogging-block a necessary station on the road to perfection, and who ended a sermon on the Sixth Beatitude by saying, "Now boys, be pure in heart! For if not, I'll flog you until you are!"

The country gentlemen and merchant princes who put their sons under his care were not displeased by such a specimen of pious ferocity, nor could they think lightly of the man who had birched half the ministers, bishops, generals, and dukes in the kingdom.

In those days the severest discipline found favour with the best people. The recent French Revolution had proved the dangers of liberalism when it affects the governing classes. Official

1

England, which was the soul of the Holy Alliance, believed that in combating Napoleon she was combating liberalism in the purple. She required from her public schools a generation of smooth-tongued hypocrites.

In order to crush out any possible republican ardour in the young aristocrats of Eton, their studies were organized on conventional and frivolous lines. At the end of five years the pupil had read Homer twice through, almost all Virgil, and an expurgated Horace; he could turn out passable Latin epigrams on Wellington and Nelson. The taste for Latin quotations was then so pronounced, that Pitt in the House of Commons being interrupted in a quotation from the *Æneid,* the whole House, Whigs and Tories alike, rose as one man to supply the end. Certainly a fine example of homogeneous culture.

The study of science, being optional, was naturally neglected, but dancing was obligatory. On the subject of religion Keate held doubt to be a crime, but that otherwise it wasn't worth talking about. He feared mysticism more than indifference, permitted laughing in chapel and wasn't strict about keeping the Sabbath.

Here, in order to make the reader understand the—perhaps unconscious—Machiavelism of this celebrated trainer of youth, we may note that he

2

did not mind being told a few lies: "A sign of respect," he would say.

Barbarous customs reigned amongst the boys themselves. The little boys were the slaves or "fags" of the big boys. The fag made his master's bed, fetched from the pump outside and carried up his water in the morning, brushed his clothes, and cleaned his shoes. Disobedience was punished by torments to fit the crime. A boy writing home, not to complain, but to describe his life, says: "Rolls, whose fag I am, put on spurs to force me to jump a ditch which was too wide for me. Each time I funked it he dug them into me, and of course my legs are bleeding, my 'Greek Poets' reduced to pulp, and my new clothes torn to tatters."

The glorious "art of self-defence" was in high honour. At the conclusion of one strenuous bout, a boy was left dead upon the floor. Keate, coming to look at the corpse, said simply: "This is regrettable, of course, but I desire above all things that an Eton boy should be ready to return a blow for a blow."

The real, but hidden, aim of the system was to form "hard-faced men," all run in the same mould. In action you might be independent, but any originality of thought, of dress, or of language was the most heinous of crimes. To betray the smallest interest in ideas or books was a bit of disgusting affectation to be forcibly pulled up by the roots.

Such a life as this seemed to the majority of English boys quite right. The pride they felt in carrying on the traditions of a school like Eton founded by a king, and under the protection of and near neighbour to all the succeeding kings, was balm of Gilead to their woes.

Only a few sensitive souls suffered terribly and suffered long.

One of these, for example, the young Percy Bysshe Shelley, son of a rich Sussex landowner, and grandson to Sir Bysshe Shelley, Bart., did not seem able to acclimatize himself at all.

This boy, who was exceptionally beautiful, with brilliant blue eyes, dark curling hair, and a delicate complexion, displayed a sensitiveness of conscience most unusual in one of his class, as well as an incredible tendency to question the Rules of the Game.

When first he appeared in the school, the Sixth Form captains, seeing his slender build and girlish air, imagined they would have little need to enforce their authority over him. But they soon discovered that the smallest threat threw him into a passion of resistance. An unbreakable will, with a lack of the necessary physical strength to carry out its decrees, forefated him to rebellion. His eyes, dreamy when at peace, acquired, under the influence of enthusiasm or indignation, a light that was almost wild; his voice, usually soft and low, became agonized and shrill.

His love of books, his contempt for games, his long hair floating in the wind, his collar opened on a girlish throat, everything about him scandalized those self-charged to maintain in the little world of Eton the brutal spirit of which it was so proud.

But Shelley, from his first day there, having decided that fagging was an outrage to human dignity, had refused obedience to the orders of his fag-master, and in consequence was proclaimed an outlaw.

He was called "Mad Shelley." The strongest of his tormentors undertook to save his soul as by fire, although they gave up attacking him in single combat, when they found he would stop at nothing. Scratching and slapping, he fought with open hands like a girl.

An organized "Shelley-bait" became one of the favourite amusements. Some scout would discover the strange lad reading poetry by the riverside, and at once give the "view hallo!" Shelley, with his hair streaming on the wind, would take flight across the meadows, through the college cloisters, the Eton streets. Finally, surrounded like a stag at bay, he would utter a prolonged and piercing shriek, while his tormentors would "nail" him to the wall with balls slimey with mud.

A voice would cry "Shelley!" And "Shelley!" another voice would take it up. The old walls would re-echo to yells of "Shelley!" in every key. A lickspittle fag would pluck at the victim's jacket; another would pinch him; a third would kick away the books he squeezed convulsively under his arm. Then, every finger would be pointed towards him, while fresh cries of "Shelley!" "Shelley!" "Shelley!" finally shattered his nerves.

The crisis was reached for which his tormentors waited—an outburst of mad rage, in which the boy's eyes flashed fire, his cheeks grew white, his whole body trembled and shook.

Tired at length of a spectacle that was always the same, the school went back to its games.

Shelley picked up his mud-stained books and, lost in thought, wandered away through the meadows that border the Thames and, flinging himself down on the sun-flecked grass, watched the river glide past him. Running water, like music, has the power to change misery into melancholy. Both, through their smooth, unceasing flow, pour over the soul the anodyne of forgetfulness and peace. The massive towers of Windsor and Eton typified to the young rebel a hostile and unchanging world, but the reflection of the willow-trees trembling in the water soothed him by its tenuous fragility.

He returned to his books, to Diderot, to Voltaire, to the system of M. d'Holbach. To love these Frenchmen, so hated by his masters, seemed an act of defiance worthy of his courage. An English work condensed them all. Godwin's *Political Justice*. It was his favourite reading.

Godwin made all things seem simple. Had men studied him the world would have attained to a state of idyllic happiness. Had they listened to the voice of reason, that is of Godwin, two hours' work a day would have been sufficient for all their needs. Free love would have replaced the stupid conventions of marriage, and philosophy have banished the terrors of superstition.

Unfortunately, "prejudices" still shut men's minds to truth.

Shelley closed his book, stretched himself out upon the sunny, flower-starred grass, and meditated on the misery of man. From the school buildings behind him a confused murmur of stupid voices floated out over the exquisite landscape of wood and stream, but here at least no mocking eye could spy upon him. The boy's tears ran down, and pressing his hands together, he made this vow: "I swear to be just and wise and free, if such power in me lies. I swear never to become an accomplice, even by my silence, of the selfish and the powerful. I swear to dedicate my whole life to the worship of beauty."

Had Dr. Keate been witness to an outburst of religious ardour so deplorable in any well-regulated school, he would certainly have treated the case in his favourite way.

CHAPTER II

THE HOME

IN the holidays the refractory slave became the hereditary prince. Mr. Timothy Shelley, his father, owned the manor of Field Place in Sussex, a well built, low, white house surrounded by a park, and extensive woods. There Shelley found his four pretty sisters, a little brother three years old, whom he had taught to say "The devil!" so as to shock the pious, and his beautiful cousin Harriet Grove, who people said resembled him.

The head of the family, Sir Bysshe Shelley, lived in the market-town of Horsham. He was a gentleman of the old school who boasted of being as rich as a duke and of living like a poacher. Six feet high, of commanding presence and a handsome face, Sir Bysshe was of cynical mind and energetic temperament. The Shelleys inherited their brilliant blue eyes from him.

He had sunk eighty thousand pounds in building Castle Goring, but could not finish it because of the expense. So he lived in a cottage close to the Horsham Town Hall, with one man-servant as eccentric as himself. He dressed like a peasant and spent his days in the tap-room of the Swan Inn, talking politics with all and sundry. From America he had brought back a rough humour that frightened the slow-witted country-folk. He had made his two daughters so unhappy at home that they had run away, which afforded him an excellent pretext for not giving them any dowry.

His one desire was to round off an immense estate and to transmit it intact to innumerable generations of Shelleys. With this in view he had entailed the greater part of it on Percy, to the total exclusion of his other children. Considering his grandson as the necessary upholder of his posthumous ambition, he had a certain affection for him. But for his son Timothy, who dealt in stilted phrases, he had nothing but contempt.

Timothy Shelley was member of Parliament for the pocket borough of New Shoreham. Like his father, he was tall and well made, fair, handsome and imposing. He had a better heart than Sir Bysshe but less will-power. Sir Bysshe was attractive enough, as avowed egoists and cynics often are. Timothy had good intentions and was insupportable. He admired intellect with
10

the irritating want of tact of the illiterate. He affected a fashionable respect for religion, an aggressive tolerance for new ideas, a pompous philosophy. He liked to call himself liberal in his political and religious opinions, but was careful not to scandalize the people of his set. A friend of the Duke of Norfolk, he spoke with complacency of the emancipation of the Irish Catholics. He was proud of his own boldness and not a little scared by it. He had tears at command, but became ferocious if his vanity was touched. In private life he plumed himself on his urbanity, but tried to combine the mailed fist with the velvet glove. Diplomatic in small things he was boorish in big ones; inoffensive yet exasperating, he was well fitted to try the temper of any young critic; and it was the vexation caused by the silly bibble-babble of his father which had done much to throw Shelley into intellectual isolation. As to Mrs. Shelley, she had been the prettiest girl in the county, she liked a man to be a fighter, and she would watch with disgust her eldest son go off into the woods carrying a book under his arm instead of a gun.

In the eyes of his sisters, however, Shelley was a Superman. The moment he arrived from Eton the house was filled with fantastic guests, the park was alive with confused murmurs as in "A

Midsummer Night's Dream." The little girls lived in a continual but agreeable terror. Percy delighted in clothing with mystery the everyday objects of life. There was no hole in the old walls into which he did not thrust a stick in the search for secret passages. In the attics he had discovered a locked room. Here, said he, lived an old alchemist with a long beard, the terrible Cornelius Agrippa. When a noise was heard in the attics, it was Cornelius upsetting his lamp. During a whole week the Shelley family worked in the garden, digging out a summer shelter for Cornelius.

Other monsters woke again with the boy's arrival. There was the great tortoise which lived in the pond, and the great old snake, a formidable reptile, that once had really frequented the underwood, and which one of the Squire's gardeners had killed with a scythe. "This gardener, little girls, this gardener who had the look of a human being like you and me, was in reality Father Time himself who causes all legendary monsters to perish."

What rendered these inventions so fascinating was that the teller himself was not too sure he was inventing them. Stories of witches and ghosts had troubled his sensitive childhood. But the more he feared ghostly apparitions the more

12

he forced himself to brave them. At Eton, having drawn a circle on the ground, and set fire to some alcohol in a saucer, which enveloped him in its bluish flame, he began his incantation: "Demons of the air, and of fire. . . ." "What on earth are you doing, Shelley?" said his Master, the solemn and magnificent Bethel, interrupting him one day: "Please, sir, I'm raising the devil. . . ." In the country likewise the Lord of Darkness was often called up by a shrill young voice, and sometimes to their great joy the children received an order from the sovereign brother to dress up as ghosts or demons.

The discipline of science was quite alien to Shelley's nature, but he liked its romantic side. Armed with a machine which had just been invented, he gave electric shocks to the admiring bevy of little girls. But whenever little Hellen, the youngest, saw him coming with a bottle and a bit of wire she began to cry.

His dearest and most faithful disciples were Elizabeth his eldest sister, and his lovely cousin, Harriet Grove. These three children were drawn together by their dawning senses and their impassioned love of Truth. The awakening of instinct always sheds over ideas an extraordinary charm. Shelley led his fair pupils to the churchyard to which the mysterious presence of the dead lent, in his eyes, a poetic fascination, and safe from the pursuit of his father, seated between them on some rustic tomb in the shadow of the old church, arms round swaying waists, he discoursed eloquently on all things in heaven and earth while lovely eyes drank up his every word.

The picture he drew of the world was a simple one. On the one side Vice: kings, priests, and the rich. On the other Virtue: philosophers, the wretched, and the poor. Here, religion in the service of tyranny: there, Godwin and his *Political Justice*. But more often he spoke to the girls of Love.

"Men's laws pretend to regulate our natural sentiments. How absurd! When the eye perceives a lovely being the heart takes fire. How is it under man's control to love or not to love? But the essence of love is liberty and it withers in an atmosphere of constraint. It is incompatible with obedience, jealousy, or fear. It requires perfect confidence and absolute freedom. Marriage is a prison. . . ."

Scepticism extended to marriage is a form of wit which unmarried ladies do not much appreciate. Metaphysical heresy may sometimes amuse them, matrimonial heresy smells of the faggot.

14

"Bonds?" repeated Harriet. "No doubt. . . . But what matter if the bonds are light ones?"

"If they are light they are useless. Does one shackle a voluntary prisoner?"

"But religion . . ."

Shelley called Holbach to the aid of Godwin. "If God is just, how can we believe that he will punish creatures whom he himself has created weak? If he is All-Powerful how is it possible either to offend him or resist him? If he is reasonable, why is he angry with the hapless beings to whom he has left the liberty to be unreasonable?"

"Custom . . ."

"What can custom matter to us in this short moment of eternity which we call the nineteenth century?"

Elizabeth took her brother's side, and it was impossible for Harriet to oppose a demigod with flashing eyes, a shirt-collar open on a delicate throat, and hair as fine as spun-silk.

She sighed; then to change the conversation, "Let us go on with *Zastrozzi?*" she proposed.

This was a novel which the three were writing together. It dealt with a robber chief, a haughty tyrant, and an "elegantly proportioned heroine all tenderness and purity."

The hours passed pleasantly in *Zastrozzi's*

15

company; the evening closed in. Elizabeth left the guileless lovers alone in the darkness.

Shelley and Harriet, their arms interlocked, wandered back to the house through the white mist rising from the meadows. The breeze waved the topmost leaves of the trees across the face of the moon. The anemones shut their pale cups and drooped their heads. The sadness of twilight reminded Shelley of his approaching return to the sombre cloisters of Eton. But conscious of the warm loveliness of his cousin, who trembled and vibrated beneath his touch, he felt himself filled with new courage for a life of apostleship and combat.

CHAPTER III

IN October, 1810, Timothy Shelley took his son up to Oxford. The member for New Shoreham was in the best of tempers.

Mr. Shelley had come to enter a future baronet in the books of University College; through which he himself had passed many years earlier, without distinction. Such ceremonies are always agreeable to an Englishman, and would be particularly so to a man of the consequential turn of mind of Timothy Shelley. So soon as the rite was satisfactorily accomplished, he went down with Bysshe to the bookseller, and there opened for him an unlimited credit in books and paper.

"My son here," he said, pointing good-humouredly to the wild-haired youth with luminous eyes who stood by, "has a literary turn, Mr. Slatter. He is already the author of a romance" —it was the famous *Zastrozzi*—"and if he wishes to publish again, do pray indulge him in his printing freaks."

17

Shelley was delighted with college. To have rooms of his own, where he could sport his oak; to be free to attend lectures or shirk them; to follow the studies of his choice; to read, write, or go walking as he pleased; this was to combine the charm of the monastic life with the freedom of thought of the philosopher. It was thus he had dreamed of passing his life "for ever."

That evening in the hall he found himself seated by the side of a young man, also a freshman, who after introducing himself as "Jefferson Hogg" relapsed into the high-bred reserve which Oxford manners require. However, towards the middle of the meal the two young men, incapable of maintaining silence any longer, began to talk of their reading.

"The best poetical literature of these days," said Shelley, "is German literature."

Hogg, with a smile, asserted the German's want of nature. So much romanticism made him tired. . . .

"What modern literature can you compare with theirs?"

Hogg named the Italian.

This roused all Shelley's impetuosity, and started such an endless discussion that the servants were able to clear the tables before the two perceived they were alone.

THE CONFIDANT

"Will you come up to my rooms?" said Hogg. "We can go on talking there."

Shelley eagerly accepted, but he lost the thread of his discourse on the way and the whole of his enthusiasm in the cause of Germany. While Hogg was lighting the candles, his guest said calmly that he was not qualified to maintain such a discussion, being as ignorant of Italian as he was of German, and that he had only talked for talking's sake.

Hogg replied smiling that his own indifference and ignorance were profound, and proceeded to set out on the table a bottle, glasses, and biscuits.

"Besides," declared Shelley, "all literature is vain trifling. What is the study of ancient or modern tongues but merely a study of words and phrases, of the names of things? How much wiser it were to investigate the things themselves!"

How was this to be done, Hogg wanted to know.

"Through the physical sciences, and especially through chemistry," said Shelley, and raising his voice he discoursed with a degree of animation that far outshone his zeal in defence of the Germans, on chemical analysis, on the recent discoveries in physics, and on electricity.

Feeling no interest in these subjects Hogg

had leisure to examine the appearance of his new friend. His clothes were expensive, and made according to the most approved mode of the day, but they were tumbled, rumpled, unbrushed. His figure was slight and fragile, he was tall, but appeared less tall than he really was, being round-shouldered, through an habitual eagerness of mood which always made him thrust his face forward. His gestures were both graceful and abrupt, his complexion red and white like a girl's; his hair dark-brown, long and bushy. His features breathed an animation, a fire, a vivid and preternatural intelligence. Nor was the moral expression less beautiful than the intellectual, for there was a softness, a delicacy, a gentleness about it, and that air of profound religious veneration which characterizes the frescoed saints of the great masters of Florence.

Shelley was still talking when some clock chimed—he uttered a cry "My mineralogy class!" and fled downstairs.

. . . .

Hogg had promised to call on him next morning. He found him in a violent dispute with the scout who wanted to tidy up his rooms.

Books, boots, papers, pistols, linen, ammunition, phials, and crucibles were scattered on the floor and on every chair and table. An electrical machine, an air pump, and a solar microscope were conspicuous amidst the mass of matter. Shelley turned the handle of the machine so that the fierce crackling sparks flew out, and presently getting upon the stool with glass feet, his long wild locks bristled and stood on end. Hogg, with a look of amusement, followed his movements with anxiety, watching in particular over the glasses and tea-cups. Just as his host was going to pour out tea, the guest removed in haste from the bottom of his cup a small gold seven-shilling piece partly dissolved by the nitromuriatic acid in which it was immersed.

The young men became inseparable. Every morning they went for a long walk, during which Shelley behaved like a child, climbing all the banks, jumping all the ditches.

When he came to any water he launched paper boats, and sent little argosies trembling down the Isis. He followed them until they sank, while Hogg, compliant but exasperated, waited for him at the starting point by the water's edge.

After the walk they went up to Shelley's rooms where, worn out by his continual expenditure of energy, he would be overcome by extreme drowsiness. He would lie stretched out upon the rug before a large fire and, curled round upon himself like a cat, would sleep thus from six to ten. At

21

ten he would suddenly start up, and rubbing his eyes with great violence and passing his fingers swiftly through his long hair, he would enter at once into a vehement argument, or begin to recite verses with an energy which was almost painful.

At eleven he supped, but his meals were very simple. Eating no meat on principle, he liked bread, and his pockets were always full of it. He would walk reading and nibbling as he went, and his path was marked by a long line of crumbs. Next to bread he liked pudding raisins and dried prunes bought at the grocers. A regular sit-down meal was intolerably boring to him, and he hardly ever remained to the end.

After supper his mind was clear and his conversation brilliant. He spoke to Hogg about his cousin Harriet, to whom he wrote long letters in which outbursts of love alternated with Godwin's philosophy; about his sister Elizabeth, a valiant enemy of convention. Or he read the last solemn letter from his father with shrieks of laughter. Or he took up one of his favourite books, Locke, Hume or Voltaire, and commented on it with enthusiasm.

Hogg often asked himself why these writers exercised so great a fascination over the religious and mystical nature of his friend. It seemed as though in suddenly discovering in the by-ways of

his extensive reading the immense variety of sys-
tems, resembling an entanglement of deep valleys
and rocky precipices, that a sort of vertigo must
have seized Shelley and only a clear and simple
doctrine such as Godwin's could relieve his metaphysical giddiness. He amused himself by sub-
stituting for the titanic and confused accumula-
tions of History, an aëry edifice of crystalline
theories, and he preferred to the real world, the
incoherence of which terrified him, the more
agreeable vision which the soul gains by looking
at facts through the vaporous meshes of clouds.

Then the college clock struck two, Hogg got
up, and in spite of the protestations of his friend
went off to bed.

"What an extraordinary creature!" thought he
as he went up to his room . . . "the grace of a
young girl, the purity of a maiden who has never
left her mother's side . . . and nevertheless an
indomitable force . . . the soul of a Benedictine
monk, with the ideas of a Jacobin."

It was certainly a strange mixture, well worth
thinking over. But Master Jefferson Hogg
didn't care about tiring his brain, and his dear
friend Shelley always gave him an overwhelming
desire to sleep.

CHAPTER IV

THE NEIGHBOURING PINE

A FEW days before Christmas Mr. Shelley found in his letter-bag a communication from a London publisher, a certain Mr. Stockdale, who called his attention to the extraordinary productions which young Mr. Percy Shelley desired to have published. Stockdale had received the MS. of a novel, *St. Irvyne, or the Rosicrucian*, filled with the most subversive ideas, and the worthy tradesman could not see without misgiving the son of so estimable a gentleman as Mr. Shelley treading this dangerous path. He considered it to be his duty to warn the young man's father; and above all to call his attention to the young man's evil genius, his comrade Mr. Jefferson Hogg, son of a good old Tory family in the north of England, but thoroughly false and dangerous in character.

Mr. Shelley replied by informing Stockdale that he refused to pay one penny of the printing bill, which greatly increased the metaphysical and doctrinal anxieties of the publisher. Then, while awaiting the arrival of his son, who was to spend the first week of the Christmas holidays at Field Place, he prepared one of his incoherent, affectionate, and blustering sermons, in the bombastic style of which he was past master.

Arguments have never convinced anybody yet. But to imagine that the arguments of a father can change the ideas of a son is the height of argumentative madness. At the close of the conversation Shelley went away sickened by the stupidity of his family, filled with a righteous fury at the behaviour of Stockdale so unworthy of a gentleman, and more than ever attached to Jefferson Hogg, his only friend. That very evening he sat down and confided everything to him in a long letter:

"Everybody attacks me for my detestable principles; I am reckoned an outcast; there lowers a terrific tempest, but I stand as it were on a pharos, and smile exultingly at the vain beating of the billows below. I attempted to enlighten my father. *Mirabile dictu!* He, for a time, listened to my arguments; he allowed the impossibility of any direct intervention of Providence. He allowed the utter incredibility of witches, ghosts, legendary miracles. But when I came *to apply* the truths on which we had agreed so harmoniously, he started . . . and silenced me with an equine argument 'I believe because I believe.'

"My mother believes me to be in the high-road to Pandemonium. She fancies I want to make a deistical coterie of all my little sisters. How laughable!"

Field Place, usually so gay during the holidays, was overshadowed by these happenings. Mrs. Shelley advised her daughters not to speak too much with Percy, and the little girls became shy and silent. They continued their Christmas preparations through force of habit, but no one took any further interest in them; the little amusements and surprises were arranged as usual, but without the laughter and fun which makes Christmas Day so delightful in happy families.

Only Elizabeth remained faithful to Shelley in secret. But she saw that her admiration was no longer shared by her cousin Harriet, who grew colder and more evasive every day.

The letters which Harriet had received from Oxford, filled with enthusiastic dissertations extremely difficult to follow, had troubled and annoyed her. The quotations from Godwin bored her to tears, and her terror was even greater than her boredom. It is rare that pretty women show a taste for dangerous ideas. Beauty, the natural expression of law and order, is conservative by essence; it upholds all established religions of which it adorns the ceremonies; Venus was always the right hand of Jupiter.

Harriet showed Shelley's letters to her mother, who advised her to pass them on to her father. This gentleman pronounced Shelley's doctrines to be abominable. Both parents took gloomy views as to the young man's future. Ought Harriet to unite herself with an eccentric creature whose follies alienated everybody? She loved elegance, county balls, and admiration. What sort of a life would she lead with this mad boy who respected nothing, not even marriage? Yet after all, religion has claims . . . .

Before Shelley's arrival the two young girls had some violent discussions. Elizabeth pleaded his cause. How could Harriet weigh a few poor worldly successes against the happiness of passing her life with the most marvellous of men?

"You make your brother out to be an extraordinary person, but how can I be sure he really is as you represent him? We have always lived in the country, we know nothing of life. Our parents, your own father even, who is in Parliament, disapprove of Bysshe's ideas. However, let us admit that he is a genius. What right have *I* to enter into an intimacy with him which must end in disappointment when he discovers how really inferior I am to the being his imagination has pictured? I am just an ordinary young girl like all the rest. He has idealized me and he would be very much surprised if he knew me as I am."

So much modesty gives one to think: Love does not reason like this.

When Shelley arrived Elizabeth explained the situation to him. Instantly he sought Harriet out. He found her cold and distant, exactly as Elizabeth had described her. She did not ask Shelley to justify himself: all she asked was that he should leave her alone. She reproached him with his universal scepticism.

"But really, Harriet," Shelley protested, "it is monstrous that I should not be allowed to express opinions which I have reached by the most logical of arguments. And how can my theological opinions disqualify me as brother, friend, or lover?"

"You may think what you please," replied Harriet, "I do not care in the least what you think, but don't ask me to unite my lot with yours."

It was the first time Shelley had come in contact with a woman's indifference, which she can sprmg upon a man with the suddenness of night falling in the centre of Africa.

He went away mad with grief. Through the naked, frozen woods, he wandered back towards Field Place; unconscious of the drifting snow, he paced for hours the village graveyard, which had been the background for love's young dream.

He got home at two o'clock in the morning, and went to bed after placing a loaded pistol, and various poisons taken from his chemical arsenal, by his side. But the thought of Elizabeth's grief on finding his corpse, prevented him from killing himself.

Next day he wrote to Hogg. Against Harriet herself he expressed no resentment, none against his father **nor** Mr. Grove. The Spirit of Intolerance alone was responsible for the tragedy:

"Here I swear—and as I break my oaths, may Infinity, Eternity blast me—I swear that I will never forgive Intolerance! It is the only point on which I allow myself to encourage revenge; every moment I can spare shall be devoted to my object. Intolerance is of the greatest disservice to Society; it encourages prejudices which strike at the root of the dearest, the tenderest of its ties. Oh, how I wish I were the avenger!—that it were mine to crush the demon; to hurl him to his native hell, never to rise again and thus to establish for ever perfect and universal toleration.

"I expect to gratify some of this insatiable feeling in poetry. You shall see, you shall hear, how it has injured me. *She* is no longer mine! *She* abhors me as a sceptic, as what *she* was before! O bigotry! When I pardon this last, this severest of thy persecutions, may Heaven—if there be wrath in Heaven—blast me!

"Forgive me, I have done. I am afraid there is selfishness in the passion of love, for I cannot avoid feeling every instant as if my soul were bursting. But I *will* feel no more. It is selfish. I would feel for others, but for myself—oh how much rather would I expire in the struggle! Yes, that were a relief! Is suicide wrong? I slept with a loaded pistol and some poison last night, but did not die. Had it not been for my sister, for *you*, I should have bidden you a final farewell."

There still remained a fortnight of the holidays to be passed at Field Place, an unhappy fortnight owing to the displeasure of his father and mother, and the embarrassment of his sisters.

In spite of Elizabeth's invitations Harriet

refused to come over and see them while he was there.

People began to whisper, under the seal of secrecy, that she was engaged to some one else.

Seeking to appease his spirit in the endeavour to make others happy, Shelley had resolved that Hogg should fall in love with Elizabeth, whom he had never seen. He sent Hogg some verses written by her, which were filled with good intentions, hatred of tyranny, and faults of prosody.

"All are brethren," sang Elizabeth like the good pupil she was, "even the African bending to the stroke of the hard-hearted Englishman's rod" . . . and more in the same strain.

In return, Shelley gave his sister Hogg's poems which he declared to be "extremely beautiful," and in which he himself was compared to a young oak, and Harriet Grove to the ivy which stifles the tree by its embraces.

"You have not said," wrote Shelley, "that the ivy after it had destroyed the oak, as if to mock the miseries which it had caused, twined around a pine which stood near."

The neighbouring pine was Mr. Heylar, a wealthy landowner, and a man of sound doctrines, who had been expressly created by Providence to escort his wife to county balls.

"She is lost to me for ever! She is married! Married to a clod of earth! She will become as insensible herself. All those fine capabilities will moulder. Let us speak no more on the subject."

He would have liked to invite Hogg to Field Place, so that Elizabeth might judge for herself of his admirable qualities. But the squire, remembering Stockdale's warnings concerning a certain Evil Genius, forbade the invitation.

CHAPTER V

QUOD ERAT DEMONSTRANDUM

ABOUT a month after these unfortunate holidays, Messrs. Munday & Slatter, the Oxford booksellers to whom Timothy Shelley had recommended the literary freaks of his son, saw that young man burst into their shop, his hair flying, his shirt-collar wide open, and a fat parcel of pamphlets under his arm. He wished these to be sold at sixpence each, and to be displayed conspicuously in the shop-window. To be sure of this being well done, he set about doing it himself.

The booksellers watched him at work with the amused and fatherly benevolence which Oxford tradesmen show to Oxford freshmen who have plenty of money. Had they looked closer they would have been horrified at the explosive matter with which their young customer strewed their counters and windows.

The title of the pamphlet, *The Necessity of Atheism,* was the most scandalous imaginable in a mealy-mouthed, theological city like Oxford. It was signed by the unknown name of "Jeremiah Stukeley," and had Messrs. Munday & Slatter turned over its pages they would have been more horrified still by the insolent logic of the imaginary Stukeley.

"A close examination of the validity of the proofs adduced to support any proposition, has ever been allowed to be the only sure way of attaining truth, upon the advantages of which it is unnecessary to descant."

It was with this bold axiom that the pamphlet began, and written in the form of a geometrical theorem it proceeded to prove the impossibility of the existence of God. It ended triumphantly with the three letters Q. E. D. *quod erat demonstrandum.*

To Shelley, who understood nothing of mathematics, this formula had always seemed like a magician's spell for the evocation of Truth. Although he had an ardent belief in a Spirit of universal Goodness, the creator and director of all things; although he professed the personal theology of an anglican *"Vicaire Savoyard";* the word "Atheist" pleased him because of its vigour. He loved to fling it in the face of Bigotry. He picked up the epithet with which he had already been pelted at Eton, as a Knight Errant picks up a glove. To the physical and moral courage of his race, he added intellectual courage, thus affronting great dangers and an inevitable scandal.

The Necessity of Atheism had been published just twenty minutes, when the Rev. John Walker, a Fellow of New College, a man of a sinister and inquisitorial turn of mind, passed the shop-window and looked in.

The Necessity of Atheism! . . . Astounded and outraged, the Rev. John strode into the shop, calling out in stentorian tones, "Mr. Munday! Mr. Slatter! What is the meaning of this?"

"Really, sir, we know nothing about it. We have not personally examined the pamphlet. . . ."

"*The Necessity of Atheism!* . . . But the title in itself is sufficient to inform you."

"Quite so, sir. Quite so. And now that our attention has been called to it . . ."

"Now that your attention, gentlemen, has been called to it, you will have the goodness to withdraw immediately every copy from your window, and to carry them, as well as any other copies you may possess, into your kitchen and throw them all into the fire."

Mr. Walker had not, of course, the smallest right to give any such order, but the booksellers knew that he had only to complain to the University authorities, and they would see their shop put out of bounds. So they obeyed with obsequious smiles, and sent one of their clerks to beg young Mr. Shelley to step round for a few minutes' conversation with them.

"We are very sorry, Mr. Shelley, very sorry indeed, but really we couldn't help ourselves. Mr. Walker insisted on it, and in your own interest. . . ."

But his "own interest" was the last thing Shelley ever thought of. In his piercing, urgent voice, he asserted to the much-worried booksellers his right to think as he pleased, and to communicate his thoughts to the world.

"And," he told them triumphantly, "I have done worse than spread my net in the sight of callow Oxford birds. I have sent a copy of *The Necessity of Atheism* to every bishop on the Bench, to the Chancellor of the University, and to every college Master, Warden, and Dean, with the compliments of 'Jeremiah Stukeley' in my own handwriting!"

.   .   .   .

A few days later a porter appeared in Hogg's rooms with the Dean's compliments to Mr. Shelley, and would he go down to him immediately. He went down to the Common Room where he found the Master and several of the Fellows; a little group of learned puritans, all classical and muscular Christians who had always abhorred Shelley because of his long hair, his eccentricities of dress, and his really low taste for experimental science.

The Dean showed him a copy of *The Necessity of Atheism,* and asked him if he were the author. As he spoke in a rude, abrupt, and insolent voice, Shelley did not reply.

"Are you, yes or no, the author of this pamphlet?"

"If you can prove that it is by me, produce your evidence. It is neither just nor lawful to interrogate me in this fashion. Such proceedings would become a court of inquisitors, but not free men in a free country."

"Do you choose to deny that this is your composition?"

"I refuse to reply."

"Then you are expelled, and I desire that you will quit the college to-morrow morning at the very latest."

An envelope sealed with the college seal was immediately handed to him by one of the Fellows. It contained the sentence of expulsion.

Shelley dashed back to Hogg's rooms, flung himself down on the sofa, and trembling with rage repeated "Expelled! . . . Expelled!

The punishment was terrible. It put a stop to his studies; made it impossible for him to enter any other university; deprived him of the peaceful life he so much enjoyed; and drew down on his head his father's grotesque and inextinguishable anger.

Hogg was as indignant as his friend, and carried away by a youthful generosity, instantly addressed a note to the Master and Fellows, expressing his grief and astonishment that such treatment could have been meted out to such a man as Shelley. He trusted that the sentence was not final.

The note was dispatched. The Conclave was still sitting. In a moment the porter returned with "the Dean's compliments to Mr. Hogg and would he go down at once."

The audience was brief.

"Did you write this?"

It was the letter he had just written and he acknowledged it.

"And this?" putting into Hogg's hand the pamphlet on Atheism.

With a wealth of arguments and the subtleties of a K.C., Hogg pointed out the absurdity of the question, and the injustice of punishing Shelley for having refused to answer it, the obligation lying on every man conscious of his rights. . . .

QUOD ERAT DEMONSTRANDUM

"That's enough!" shouted the Master in a furious voice. "You're expelled too!" . . . He seemed in a mood to have expelled every man in the college. Hogg was handed the sealed envelope in his turn.

In the course of the day a large official paper was affixed to the door of hall. It was signed by the Master and Dean, bore the college seal, and declared that Thomas Jefferson Hogg and Percy Bysshe Shelley were publicly expelled for refusing to answer certain questions put to them.

CHAPTER VI

TIMOTHY SHELLEY'S VIGOROUS DIALECTICS

THE exiles set off bag and baggage in the Oxford coach. Shelley had borrowed £20 from his booksellers, in order to pay his way in London while waiting news from his father.

Every lodging which he visited with Hogg appeared to him impossible, either the street was too noisy, the district too dirty, the maidservant too plain. Finally, the name of Poland Street reminded him of Warsaw, of Freedom. He was certain that in Poland Street any one of the rooms must be worthy of a free man's choice, and the very first which he visited, where there was a trellised paper, vine leaves, and huge bunches of green and purple grapes, seemed to him the most beautiful room in the world.

"Here we will settle down," said he, "and begin our Oxford days over again, our readings by the fireside, our rambles, our delightful experiences. Here we will live for ever."

Nothing was wanting to this programme but

the consent of the two fathers, Mr. Shelley and
Mr. Hogg.

. . . .

When Timothy Shelley heard of the events at
Oxford, he was enraged beyond measure. Evidently, for a wealthy landowner, a Member of
Parliament, and a J.P. for his county, it was a
most disagreeable occurrence. The accusation of
atheism annoyed him most, because he himself
was known as a Liberal, and such advanced
thought in politics required to balance it orthodoxy in religion.

He sat down and wrote a solemn letter to Mr.
Hogg, senior, deploring "the unfortunate affair
that has happened to my son and yours at Oxford," and urging him to get his "young man
home" as soon as possible. "As to me," he added,
"I shall recommend mine to read Paley's *Natural
Theology*: it is extremely applicable. I shall
read it with him."

Then he wrote a second letter to his own
"young man," very strongly worded: "Though
I have felt as a father and sympathized in the
misfortune which your criminal opinions and im-
proper acts have begot: yet you must know that
I have a duty to perform to my own character,
as well as to your young brother and sisters.

Above all my feelings as a Christian require from me a firm and decided conduct toward you.

"If you shall require aid or assistance from me—or any protection—you must pledge yourself to me:

"1st. To go immediately to Field Place, and to abstain from all communication with Mr. Hogg for some considerable time.

"2nd. That you shall place yourself under the care and society of such gentleman as I shall appoint, and attend to his instructions and directions he shall give."

If these conditions were not accepted Timothy Shelley would abandon his son to all the misery which such wicked and diabolical opinions justly entail.

Shelley's reply was brief:

"MY DEAR FATHER,

"As you do me the honour of requesting to hear the determination of my mind as the basis of your future actions I feel it my duty, although it gives me pain to wound 'the sense of duty to your own character, to that of your family and your feelings as a Christian,' decidedly to refuse my assent to both the proposals in your letter and to affirm that similar refusals will always be the fate of similar requests. With many thanks for your great kindness,

"I remain your affectionate, dutiful son,

"PERCY B. SHELLEY."

．　　．　　．　　．　　．　　．　　．　　．

The chief obstacle in the diplomatic relations between father and son is that the former desires above all things to avoid a rupture, which renders disciplinary measures difficult. His "conditions" having been succinctly refused, Timothy Shelley found himself at a loss what to do.

Not a bad man at bottom, he believed in the powerful persuasion of a bottle of old port. He resolved to go up to town and to invite the delinquents to dinner at Miller's Hotel, where the wine was good.

"After all," he said to himself, while waiting for the two young men, "one must treat young people with good humour, and even go so far, ridiculous as it may seem, as to discuss things with them. . . . A ripened and thoughtful mind should get the better, without any difficulty, of a philosopher of eighteen, and serious misfortunes may be avoided, by a word of wisdom in the nick of time. . . . I mustn't forget that Percy is my heir and that he will succeed to the title: he must be led back into the fold."

And the excellent man, while marshalling into

order Paley's chief arguments, rubbed his hands with satisfaction.

Meanwhile, the friends going on foot from Poland Street to Southwark, read aloud to each other passages from Voltaire's *Philosophical Dictionary* which Shelley had picked up on a stall. They found it extremely amusing and laughed immoderately at the old Frenchman's ridicule of the Jewish people, the intolerance with which the Bible is packed, and Jehovah's sickening and useless cruelties.

When they reached the hotel, a certain Mr. Graham, the factotum of Timothy Shelley, was already there with his friend and patron. Mr. Shelley received Hogg with a wheedling benevolence, then turning to his son, began to talk in an odd, unconnected manner, punctuating his discourse with dramatic gestures, which appeared highly ridiculous to the two young men.

"What do you think of my father?" Shelley whispered to Hogg.

"Oh, it is not your father. It is the God of the Jews, the Jehovah you have been reading about."

Percy gave a wild demoniacal burst of laughter, slipped from his seat and fell on his back at full length on the floor.

"What's the matter, Bysshe? Are you ill?

44

Are you mad? Why do you laugh?" asked his father, scandalized.

Fortunately, at the same moment dinner was announced and proving excellent, the conversation became almost cordial. When the dessert was put on the table, the squire sent his son off to order the post-horses for the next morning, while he undertook the conquest of Hogg.

"You are a very different person, sir, from what I expected to find; you are a nice, moderate, reasonable, pleasant gentleman. Tell me what you think I ought to do with my poor boy? He is rather wild, is he not?"

"Yes, rather."

"Then what am I to do?"

"If he had married his cousin he would perhaps have been less so. . . . He wants somebody to take care of him; a good wife. What if he were married?"

"But how can I do that? It is impossible. If I were to tell Bysshe to marry a girl he would refuse immediately. I know him so well."

"I have no doubt he would refuse if you were to order him to marry, and I should not blame him. But if you were to bring him in contact with some young lady who you believed would make him a suitable wife, without saying anything about marriage, perhaps he would take a

45

fancy to her, and if he did not like her you could try another."

Mr. Graham, interposing, said it was an excellent plan, and the two men talking in low voices were going over a list of the young women of their acquaintance, when Shelley returned. His father ordered a bottle of a still older port than any they had yet had, and began to speak in praise of himself. He was so highly respected in the House of Commons; he was respected by the whole House and by the Speaker in particular, who said to him, "Mr. Shelley, I do not know what we should do without you." He was greatly beloved in the county; he was an admirable Justice of the Peace; he told a very long story of how he had lately committed two poachers: "You know the fellows, Graham: You know what they are?" Graham assented. "Well, when they got out of prison, one of them came and thanked me."

Why the poacher was so grateful for a pitiless sentence Hogg never knew, for the worthy magistrate believing the wine to have by now produced its effect, attacked the principal subject of his thoughts.

"There is certainly a God," said he. "There can be no doubt of the existence of a Deity; none whatever."

46

Nobody present expressed any doubt.

"You, sir," said he, addressing himself to Hogg, "you have no doubt on the subject, have you?"

"None whatever."

"If you have, I can prove it to you in a moment."

"But I have no doubt."

"Ah . . . still you might perhaps like to hear my argument?"

"Very much."

"I will read it to you then.

He searched in all his pockets, pulling out various bills and letters, producing finally a half-sheet of note-paper, which he began to read. Bysshe listened with profound attention.

"I have heard this argument before," said he, at the end of a few minutes, and turning to Hogg, "Where have I heard that?"

"They are Paley's arguments."

"Yes," the reader observed with much complacency. "They are Paley's arguments. I copied them out of Paley's book this morning, but Paley had them originally from me; everything in Paley's book he had from me."

On this he folded up the paper, and returned it to his pocket. His son watched him with more disdain than ever, and the dinner terminated

47

without having brought about a reconciliation. Shelley refused to go with his father. His father refused to give him a penny. The only two who seemed satisfied with one another were Hogg and his host. Timothy Shelley had found his son's friend to be far more human than his son. He was not like Percy always with bristling quills, always on the strain, always dug in behind principles which one could not attack without wounding his infernal pride. Young as he was, Hogg understood life. His notions on marriage were sensible. Hogg, on his side, declared that though the oratorical eloquence of the member for New Shoreham was certainly a bit foggy, nevertheless he was very hospitable and a good sort.

A few days later he gave another proof that he understood life by making up his quarrel with his own father, who, head of a True Blue Tory family, well known for its orthodoxy, had no need to display the same horror at the actions of his "young man" as had the Whig owner of Field Place.

Hogg senior advised his son to read for the Bar and got him into a conveyancer's chambers at York. Hogg was, therefore, obliged to abandon Shelley in the Poland Street lodgings, a wistful, bright-eyed fox in the midst of the green and purple bunches of grapes.

CHAPTER VII

AN ACADEMY FOR YOUNG LADIES

ALONE in London, without friends, work, or money, Shelley fell into despair. He passed his time in writing melancholy poems, or letters to Hogg. Not knowing what to do with his evenings he went to bed at eight o'clock. Sleep alone stopped him from going over and over the story of his woes. The moment he let himself think, the image of his beautiful and shallow-hearted cousin rose to torture him. He tried to steel his heart against the painful vision by syllogisms.

"I loved a being," he told himself. "The being whom I loved is not what she was: consequently, as love appertains to mind and not to body, she exists no longer. . . . I might as well court the worms, which the soulless body of a beloved being generates in the damp unintelligent vaults of a charnel-house."

This appeared to him such excellent logic that he was astounded it brought him no consolation.

The money question grew serious. His father gave no sign of life. Shelley meeting him one day by chance, politely hoped he was well? All he got was a look black as a thunder cloud and a majestic "Your most humble servant, sir!"

Fortunately, his sisters did not forget him and sent him their pocket-money. It was all he had to live on. Elizabeth, at Field Place, was too well watched to do anything, but the younger girls were now at Mrs. Fenning's Academy for Young Ladies on Clapham Common, and very soon Mrs. Fenning's pupils made acquaintance with the fine eyes, the open shirt-collar and tossed curls of Hellen Shelley's wonderful brother.

He would arrive, his pockets bulging with biscuits and raisins, and begin to discourse on ultimate themes to an adoring circle of little girls. He had undertaken to "illuminate" the prettiest amongst them. He could not endure the idea that so much loveliness should be abandoned to "prejudices."

He admired, most of all, his sisters' greatest friend, Harriet Westbrook, a lovely child of sixteen, with light brown hair and a complexion of milk and roses. She was small, slightly and delicately formed, and had an air of youthful gaiety, of delicious freshness. She came to the rescue when Mrs. Fenning, acting on the orders of Timothy Shelley, requested Percy to visit his sisters less often. Harriet, whose family lived in Chapel Street, Mayfair, often went home: the little sisters, therefore, entrusted her with the cakes and the money intended for Percy, and she taking these to the hermit of Poland Street, the two young people became naturally the greatest friends.

Harriet Westbrook's father was a retired publican; he had made money, and desired to give his youngest daughter a genteel education. Her mother was dead, and she had been brought up by Eliza, a much older sister. One can easily imagine the interest which the Westbrook family took in the son of a baronet, the heir to an immense fortune, who was beautiful as a young god, lived in lodgings on bread and pudding raisins, and to whom the youngest of the Westbrook girls carried his sisters' pocket-money to prevent him from starving to death.

Eliza being keen to see the hero, Harriet took her with her on the next visit. Shelley was somewhat intimidated by the elder Miss Westbrook, a mature virgin, dried-up and bony, with a dead-white skin seamed with scars, and fish-like eyes that stared without intelligence, the whole crowned with an immense crop of black hair. Eliza was particularly proud of her hair. Her

51

affected manners were in striking contrast with Harriet's spontaneous gaiety. But Bysshe soon forgot she was plain when he saw that her intentions were friendly. Not only she made no objection, as might have been feared, to Harriet's visits to Poland Street, but she offered to bring her there, and on several occasions invited Shelley to come and dine with them, when Mr. Westbrook was away.

She completely won the heart of the young philosopher by asking to share with Harriet in his teaching, and undertook to read the *Philosophical Dictionary* under his guidance.

Harriet's walks with Shelley soon became the talk of the Young Ladies' Academy. One of the mistresses thought fit to warn her: "Young Mr. Shelley is notorious for his advanced opinions, and it is probable that his morals are no better than his ideas." Harriet had to give up a letter from him, filled with the most pernicious arguments, and for corresponding with an "atheist," she was threatened with expulsion. The county gentlemen's daughters gave the cold shoulder to the publican's daughter, and life in the school was made exceeding bitter to her.

One night as Shelley sat alone, reading by his fireside, a message was brought him from Eliza to say that Harriet was sick, and would he come and keep her company. He found her in bed, very pale, but lovelier than ever, with all her chestnut hair spread about her.

Old Westbrook came upstairs to say "How-d'ye-do," and Shelley was rather embarrassed on seeing him, for however free he was from convention, he could not help feeling that his presence at that late hour in a young girl's bedroom was hardly discreet.

Westbrook, however, showed himself all geniality. "Sorry I can't stop with you, but I've got friends downstairs. Perhaps you'll join us presently?"

Shelley thanked him and declined. The friends of Westbrook had no attraction for him. He sat beside Harriet's bed, with Eliza near by. She was in eloquent vein, speaking at great length on the enthralling subject of Love. Harriet complained of a headache; she could not stand the noise of conversation.

"Very well then," said Eliza, "I'll go away."

The two young things were left alone until long after midnight, while Westbrook's friends drank and roared below.

Next day Harriet was quite well.

.   .   .   .

Shelley's exile was less hard to bear from the moment he could receive the visits of a young girl and "illuminate" her soul. Nevertheless, he suffered from being separated from his sister Elizabeth. She no longer even answered his letters. Could she be shut up in her room? He determined at all costs to make a secret visit to Field Place so as to see her. At times he thought of a pacific invasion. What could happen to him, after all, if one evening he turned up there without notice, and opposed a Quaker-like silence to the cursings of his father? But the adventure was simplified when Captain Pilfold, a brother of Mrs. Shelley, offered his nephew most opportunely a jumping-off place, for his attack on Field Place.

Pilfold was a hearty and jovial old sea-dog who, under Nelson, had commanded a frigate at Trafalgar. He infinitely preferred his fantastic nephew to his solemn brother-in-law. That Percy were an atheist or not, the Captain did not care a hang. The boy had energy, and that was the important thing. He invited him to run down to Cuckfield, ten miles from Field Place, and received him with open arms.

Shelley, out of gratitude, offered to "illuminate" his host, and the Captain proved such an apt scholar that at the end of ten days he staggered the Rector and the Doctor by his fiery syllogisms.

54

At Cuckfield, Shelley made acquaintance with Miss Hitchener, a school-teacher, from the neighbouring town of Hurstpierpoint. She was rather good-looking, had a Roman nose, and was in her twenty-ninth year. She was a republican in politics, and enjoyed the reputation of being sentimental and conceited. She, on her side, lamented that there was not one who understood her. Shelley having admired, as was natural to him, the nobility of her attitude, perceived with regret that she was still a deist. He proposed "a polemical correspondence" in the course of which he would undertake to cure her of this infirmity. She agreed.

Captain Pilfold, meanwhile, set off courageously to grapple and board Timothy Shelley. He had the bright idea of enrolling in the cause the Duke of Norfolk, chief of the Whig party. Snobbism triumphed over paternal tyranny. Shelley walked back into Field Place with all the honours of war. He was given £200 a year unconditionally.

.   .   .   .

He could now again see Elizabeth, but he was overwhelmed by the change he found in her. She was livelier, and gayer, than formerly, but had become incredibly frivolous. He remembered her serious, enthusiastic; he found her apathetic to everything but dancing, trivial amusements, and silly chatter. She lived now for nothing but society.

He wished to read to her Hogg's letters as he had been used to do.

"Oh, you and your ridiculous friend! Every one I know thinks you are both mad."

On this she spoke of matrimony: she thought of little else, and nothing disgusted Shelley more. She seemed to have forgotten all they had read together on the subject, and all Godwin's elevated ideas.

"Marriage is odious and hateful," he told her. "I am sickened when I think of this despotic chain, the heaviest forged by man to shackle fiery souls. Scepticism and free love are as necessarily associated together as religion and marriage. Honourable men have no need of laws. For heaven's sake, Elizabeth, read over the Marriage Service and ask yourself if any decent man could wish the girl he loved to submit to such degradation."

"Yet you want me to marry your friend Hogg?"

"Yes, but not before a clergyman nor according to man's laws, but freely and with Love only as high priest."

"This then is the honourable advice of a brother?" said Elizabeth with disdain.

It was useless to hope to make any impression on a character become futile beyond any possible cure. "Why should I deceive myself? She is lost, lost to everything. She talks nothing but cant and twaddle. What she wants of me is that, like a fashionable brother, I should act as a jackal for husbands. Well, I refuse! I refuse emphatically."

He had returned to Field Place merely to see Elizabeth. There was no good in remaining. Invitations elsewhere were not wanting. Captain Pilfold would have been glad to have him again at Cuckfield. Westbrook was going to pass the summer in Wales, and his daughters pressed Shelley to join them. Hogg wanted him to come for a month to York; it was this last idea which tempted him most. But his father, who doubtless saw a symbolic value in the separation of the two Oxford criminals, would not have tolerated it, and as the first quarter's allowance was due on the first of September it was better to be patient. Hogg wrote jestingly that it was easy to see the lovely Harriet took precedence over old friends.

"Your jokes amuse me," Shelley answered. "If I know anything about love I am *not* in love.

But I have heard from the Westbrooks, both of whom I highly esteem."

While he still hesitated where to go, Thomas Grove, a cousin of his mother's, invited him to Cwm Elan, a wild corner of Radnorshire. Here he could economize while awaiting his allowance. He accepted the Groves' invitation.

On his way through London he would have liked to have seen Miss Hitchener and have taken her to lunch. But the school-teacher with the Roman nose feared this would not be quite a proper thing to do, there was such an immense social difference between her and Mr. Shelley. Indignant at the mere idea, Shelley wrote her a long letter on equality, in which he addressed her as "his soul's sister." Miss Hitchener began to think that Lady Shelley was a fine name and to study her reflection in the looking-glass.

CHAPTER VIII

THIS DESPOTIC CHAIN

NOW for the first time Shelley was among mountain solitudes, and heard the voices of mountain torrents, but the power of hills was not upon him. "This is most divine scenery," he wrote to Hogg, "but all very dull, stale, flat, and unprofitable; indeed, the place is a very great bore." Sitting near some tree-shaded waterfall he passed his time in reading and re-reading the letters he received from his friends. He was the director of innumerable "souls": Miss Hitchener, the faithful Hogg, Captain Pilfold, the terror of the pious, Eliza and Harriet Westbrook, without counting many whose names are unknown.

The Westbrooks had just gone back to London when he received from Harriet a most disturbing letter. Her father insisted on her returning to Mrs. Fenning's school where she had been so miserable, where her schoolfellows had sent her to Coventry, and called her "an abandoned wretch." Rather than exist in such a prison she would kill herself. "Why live? No one loves me, and I have no one to love. Is suicide a crime in one who is useless to others and insupportable to herself? Since there is no law of God, has the law of man any right to forbid so natural an action?"

A sort of terror seized Shelley. This schoolgirl logic appeared irrefutable, and it was he who had formed her mind. How then could he answer her with calculated coldness and abandon her to death? He wrote advising firmness; before despairing she should resist, she should refuse to return to school, and he himself wrote Mr. Westbrook a letter of expostulation.

The old publican was outraged. What right had this young sprig of nobility to interfere? He had been dangling after the Westbrook girls for six months or more, and Eliza imagined he would marry Harriet, but when had a future baronet ever married the daughter of a tavern-keeper? The young fellow wanted, evidently, something very different.

Westbrook had sized him up the evening he had first met him in Harriet's bedroom. He had invited him to come down and take a glass in the parlour, and Mr. Shelley had refused with disdain.

60

THIS DESPOTIC CHAIN

How could the grandson of Sir Bysshe Shelley, the wealthy baronet, be a Friend of the People, or a believer in Equality? Bah! the Upper Ten were all exactly the same.

Harriet was ordered to get ready for Clapham. She wrote to Shelley again, a letter in which a somewhat less lugubrious plan replaced that of suicide. She was too miserable at home, too cruelly persecuted, but she was ready to elope with him if he would consent.

He instantly took the coach for London in indescribable agitation of mind.

That he was partly responsible for Harriet he could not doubt. He had formed her, he had inspired her with exalted courage, and the horror of injustice. It was a letter from him which had brought about her first disgrace.

But if he eloped with her how should they live? He had no profession, no prospects—and did he really love her? Could he love anyone again after the blighting of his young hopes by his cousin?

Still, Harriet was charming, and there was something intoxicating in the idea of a journey in the company of the lovely creature he had seen one night in bed, with unbound auburn hair.

It was difficult to repel even warmer ideas.

When he saw her again her face was pale, wasted, tragic.

"They have made you suffer?"

"No, no. . . ." She hesitated to say, "I suffer because I am in love with you," but her eyes, lifted to his, confessed the truth. She was madly in love with him. He had completely transformed her. Before meeting him she had had all the normal tastes of the British schoolgirl. She had adored the red coats of the military, and when she wove day-dreams the hero was always an officer. But when she dreamed of marriage the hero became a black-coated clergyman.

Shelley had overthrown all such reasonable ideals. The first time she had heard him declaim on religion or politics, she had been frightened, and made up her mind to convert him. But at the outset his logic had crushed her, and conquered by an antagonist so greatly her superior, she found nothing but pleasure in her defeat.

When he had decided not to join them in Wales, she was afraid she had lost him, and in writing to him had exaggerated her hardships in order to bring her hero back.

Shelley had little admiration for Knight Errantry, which struck him as senseless. A man has no right to devote to Woman a life which should be consecrated to the service of Humanity. But looking on Harriet's exquisite face, which a single word from him could suffuse with happiness, he gave his principles the go-by. He took her hand in his, and declared himself hers heart and soul.

A last rag of prudence made him decide against an immediate elopement. It was dangerous and needless to force events. If they tried to coerce her, she had but to make a sign to him, he would fly to her from the ends of the earth and carry her off.

Once more her face glowed with the rosy happiness of the young girl who knows she is beloved.

. . . .

But the moment he had left her, he sighed deeply and fell into embarrassment and melancholy. He wrote to describe the situation to Hogg, and Hogg replied strongly urging his friend not to elope with Harriet without marrying her first. He knew all Shelley's hostility to marriage, but he used powerful arguments. "If you don't marry her, which will suffer? You or she? Evidently she alone. It is she whom the world will scorn. It is she who must make the sacrifice of her reputation and her security. Have you the right to ask this of her?" The appeal was cleverly turned, as selfishness was of all vices the one which Shelley most despised.

But he felt too that marriage was a shameful and immoral action. The chapters in *Political Justice* against matrimonial chains stuck in his mind. It was now that some one reassured him by saying that the great Godwin himself had been married twice.

"It is evidently useless," he wrote to Hogg, "to seek by an individual example to rejuvenate the forms of society until such time as reason shall have brought about so great a change, that the reformer be no longer exposed to stoning."

At the same time he was in no hurry to apply his new tenets. Captain Pilfold invited him to Cuckfield; he knew he would see there his "soul's sister," the handsome school-teacher with the Roman nose. He desired to complete her initiation in the Truth. So, again promising Harriet to return at the first sign she should make him, he left London.

One would need to be nineteen years old, to have the smallest doubt as to what must happen. A young girl very much in love and armed with such a promise, does not long resist her heart's desire. Before a week was out an ardent message recalled Shelley to town. The tyrants insisted on delivering up Andromeda to the Scholastic Dragon!

Shelley realized that there was no help for it

but to elope with Harriet, and marry her after-wards—as soon as possible.

Next day the Edinburgh Mail Coach carried northwards these two young things whose united ages did not exceed thirty-five.

"An act of will, not an act of passion," the young Knight told himself, as he sat facing his exquisite little sweetheart, while the stage jolted and rumbled on its way.

CHAPTER IX

A VERY YOUNG COUPLE

A PAIR of young lovers, persecuted and charming, exercises a fascination which is almost irresistible. The citizens of Edinburgh, difficult to get at where their purse is concerned, could not prevent themselves from giving an amused and indulgent welcome to the young couple who arrived at their gates in such brilliant penury.

Before leaving London Shelley had borrowed a few pounds from a friend. When he got to Edinburgh he hadn't a penny left. It was useless to hope for help from his father, whom the news of his elopement must have thrown into paroxysms of rage.

However, he found a good-humoured landlord to whom he told his story; this, with Harriet's beauty, and a promise of speedy payment, induced him to give the travellers an excellent ground-floor flat in his house.

Better still, he advanced them the money they

needed to pay their way during the first few days, and to arrange the wedding, according to the simple rites of the Scottish Church. His only condition was that Shelley should treat him and his friends to a supper on the wedding night.

So it was in the midst of Edinburgh tradesmen that the grandson of Sir Bysshe ate his wedding-feast. The fumes of the wines and the spectacle of the young people, going to the heads of the guests, these honest Puritans became a trifle too wanton for Shelly's taste. The jests grew ribald. The modest Harriet blushed crimson, and Shelley rising announced that he and his wife would say good night.

A roar of laughter was the reply.

A little later there came a knock at their door. Shelley opened it to find his landlord followed by all his friends. He spoke tipsily: "It's the custom here when there's a wedding, to come up in the middle of the night and wash the bride with whisky. . . ."

"Take another step into the room, and I blow your brains out!" cried Shelley, seizing a pistol in each hand.

Perceiving that there was something dangerous in this young man who looked so like a girl, the intruders wished him a respectful good night, and tumbled precipitately downstairs.

Thus Shelley and Harriet found themselves husband and wife, free and alone in a big unknown city. They looked at each other in rapture.

A few days had sufficed to render the young husband, who in the stage had reflected with melancholy, "An act of will and not of passion," over head and ears in love.

Harriet was really delightful to look upon: always pretty, always bright, always blooming, her head well dressed, not a hair out of its place; smart, usually plain in her neatness, without a wrinkle, without a spot, she resembled some pink-and-white flower.

Without being really cultivated she was remarkably well-informed. She had read a prodigious number of books, she still read all day long, and works of a high ethical tone for choice.

Her master, who was her lover, had given her his own veneration for Virtue, and Fénelon's *Télémaque* was her favourite hero. She practised saying over the magic words "Intolerance," "Equality," "Justice," and her child-lips uttered maxims which would have staggered the Lord Chancellor. As to the Anglican religion she ignored it as completely as did Calypso and Nausicaa.

Children are delightful, but their society is fatiguing. Fully alive to the charm, sweet temper, and unselfishness of Harriet, nevertheless Shelley now and again sighed for Hogg's caustic talk, or Miss Hitchener's ardent enthusiasm. He asked himself uneasily what the latter would think of his marriage.

"My dearest Friend," he wrote her, "if I may still address you so? Or have I lost, through my equivocal conduct, the esteem of the virtuous and the wise? . . . How in one week all my plans have changed, and to what an extent are we the slaves of circumstance! You will ask how I, an atheist, could submit myself to the marriage ceremony, how my conscience could ever consent to it? This is what I want to explain to you. . . ."

Thereupon, treading in Hogg's footsteps, he proved that one has not the right to deprive a beloved being of all the advantages which are bound up with a good reputation.

"Blame if thou wilt, dearest friend, for *still* thou art dearest to me, yet pity even this error if thou blamest me. If Harriet be not at six-

teen all you are at a more advanced age, assist
me to mould a really noble soul into all that
can make its nobleness useful and lovely. . . .
Charming she is already unless I am the weakest
of error's slaves."

The letter finished with an invitation that the
lady should join them at Edinburgh, where
Harriet's presence would prevent any thought
of impropriety. Miss Hitchener did not accept.
Evidently the poetic "thee's" and "thou's" were
not sufficient to buy pardon for the somewhat
unfortunate comparison drawn between her age
and Harriet's.

But though the virgin of Cuckfield declined
to come and help in the moulding of Harriet's
soul, one sunny morning Shelley heard a knock
at the door of his flat, and looking out of the
window was overjoyed to see Hogg standing in
the street, bag in hand.

Having just given himself a few weeks' holi-
day, he came to pass them in Edinburgh. He
received a triumphal reception.

"We have met at last once more!" cried
Shelley. "And we will never part again! You
must have a bed in the house!"

Harriet came in. Hogg was charmed with
her. He had never seen such blooming, radiant

youth and beauty. The landlord was summoned.

"We want another bedroom, instantly, urgently, indispensably!" When the poor man was permitted to answer, he offered them a room at the top of the house.

The three friends had a thousand things to tell and to ask. They all talked at once, while a dirty little nymph, the servant of the house, brought in tea with many discordant ejaculations.

So soon as the excitement had subsided somewhat, Shelley proposed a walk, and they went to visit the palace of Mary Stuart.

Harriet, as an excellent pupil of the Academy for Young Ladies and a tireless reader of historical romances, explained the history of the unhappy Queen. On leaving Holyrood House Shelley declared he must go home and write letters, but he wished Hogg and Harriet to climb to Arthur's Seat, whence they would get a view of the whole city.

Hogg having admired the scene, they sat there a long time together, and probably in such delightful company he would have found any view admirable.

As they came down, the wind, having begun to blow, displayed Harriet's ankles, which Hogg by a side glance examined with interest.

This made Harriet sit down again upon a rock and declare she would remain there "for ever!"

Hogg, who was desperately hungry, protested in vain. So he left her and presently she came running down after him.

Thus began for the three young people some delightful weeks.

The money question remained an anxious one, but jolly Uncle Pilfold sent frequent presents. "To be confoundedly angry with his son is all very well, but to stop the supplies is a great deal too bad." Hogg, also, had some spare cash, although Timothy Shelley had taken the trouble to write to Hogg senior: "I think it my duty to warn you that my young man has just set off for Scotland with a young female, and that your young man has joined them."

Every morning Shelley would go out to fetch his letters, the number of which remained prodigious. After breakfast he worked at a translation of Buffon which he had undertaken, while Hogg and Harriet went for a walk. If the weather were bad she read aloud to Hogg. She was fond of reading aloud and she read remarkably well, with a very distinct enunciation and an agreeable voice.

Hogg listened to the greater part of *Télé-*

maque and never complained. The virtuous Idomeneus giving wise laws to Crete was horribly boring, but the reader was so lovely to look upon that he would have listened without complaining the whole day through.

Shelley, less polite, would sometimes drop off to sleep, and his innocent slumbers gave serious offence. His friend would support his wife in stigmatizing him as an inattentive wretch, Hogg taking an unconscious pleasure in making common cause with Harriet.

It was the year of the famous comet and of the still more famous vintage, 1811. The nights were clear and bright.

CHAPTER X

HOGG

AT the end of six weeks it was necessary that Hogg should return to York. As Shelley and Harriet had nothing to retain them in Edinburgh, nor indeed anywhere else in the world, they decided to go with him. They would remain with him in York during the year which he must still spend in that city, and then all three would remove to London where they would live "for ever" writing, reading, and being read to.

Not to overtire Harriet they hired a post-chaise. On either side of the road fields of turnips alternated monotonously with fields of barley.

"But which are the turnips and which is the barley?" Harriet asked.

"Why, you little Cockney!" Shelley, the heir to broad lands, exclaimed with indignation.

Silent in his corner, Hogg, the scoffer, asked

74

himself how it came about that the virtuous
Idomeneus had taught his disciple so little.

To while away the time, Harriet read aloud
in the chaise Holcroft's novels. The rigid, spar-
tan, iron tone of that stern author was not en-
couraging. Bysshe sometimes sighed deeply.

"Is it necessary to read all that, Harriet dear?"

"Yes, absolutely."

"Cannot you skip some part?"

"No, it is impossible."

At the first relay, Shelley vanished. He had
always possessed the astonishing power of vanish-
ing like an Elf. He was recaptured by Hogg,
who found him standing on the seashore—it was
at Berwick—gazing mournfully at the setting
sun.

He took a violent dislike to York. The
theological and civic pre-eminence of the old city
had no charm for him, and the only lodgings
they could find were dingy rooms kept by a
couple of dingy milliners in a dingy street.
"It's impossible to stay here," Bysshe declared.
But to move elsewhere money was needed.
He decided to go and see Captain Pilfold, protector of the good and free; there, too, at Cuckfield, he would again meet Miss Hitchener;
perhaps he could persuade her to go back with
him to York, and on their way through London

they could pick up Eliza Westbrook, whose company was much desired by Harriet. And thus, for the first time, all Shelley's spiritual sisters would find themselves together.

He therefore took the coach, and Harriet and Hogg were left by themselves, a strange and delicious situation. In this city, where they had no acquaintances, they were as free as on some desert island, and Harriet found a childish pleasure in playing at "housekeeping" with her young and witty companion. Hogg's sarcastic tongue amused her greatly, and was a relief to Shelley's burning seriousness which she admired so much. Hogg was always paying her compliments, both in Edinburgh and on the journey to York, and she saw no harm in it. Percy was always a little bit of "the schoolmaster." He had taught her all she knew. He gravely corrected her mistakes. He was conscious of her limitations. Hogg, on the contrary, admired everything she did, noticed her frocks, and the way she did her hair. He listened to *Télémaque,* and praised the voice of the reader. He was always gay. It was really very pleasant.

Hogg's own sentiments were quite other and less commendable. Living continually in the company of this charming girl, he began to

76

desire her with passion. At first he told himself
that the very thought of such a thing was frightful, and that the wife of his best friend could
never be an object of his pursuit. But when one
is intelligent, one knows how to put intelligence
at the service of one's desires.

"Am I to blame," said he, "if Bysshe throws
her in my arms? What a mad notion of his to
sit and write long letters on Virtue when he
possesses an adorable creature like Harriet!
For she is ravishingly pretty. When she walks
in the streets the most Puritanical run to the
windows to look at her. . . . Does Bysshe
really love her? He shows her a rather contemptuous sort of affection, and has some
excuse for it. For Harriet is . . . what? The
daughter of a publican. . . . She can't be
very? . . ."

Ever since he first knew Shelley, two con-
tradictory sentiments had divided his soul. He
admired his friend's moral courage, frankness,
and ardent loyalty. He knew him to be unique,
a diamond of the purest water. Yet, at the
same time, his sense of humour was tickled by
Percy's declamatory vehemence, by his feverish
energy that yet accomplished nothing.

At Oxford Hogg had acted the cultured
Sancho Panza to this fair-skinned Don Quixote,

and had taken his share of the punishment meted out by the terrible windmills. His admiration in the beginning had triumphed over his irony, which simply served to lend the former a more tender hue. Now, stirred up by a guilty passion, his irony visibly increased.

On the first day of Shelley's absence, when Hogg left his chambers he took Harriet for a walk by the river. He gazed in her eyes with delight, and murmured a thousand foolish things. She talked of her husband whose return she longed for, partly for his own sake but chiefly because he was to bring with him her dearest Eliza. "Eliza is very beautiful as you will see. She has splendid hair, jet black, glossy . . . she is awfully clever . . . it is she who has always guided me in the important affairs of my life."

"The child has had important affairs in its life?"

Harriet spoke of her martyrdom at school—of the obstacles to her marriage—she remained pensive a moment, plunged in the past; then, "What is your opinion of suicide? Did you ever think of destroying yourself?"

"Never! Nor you either, I should hope?"

"Oh yes, very often. Even at school I used to get up in the night with the fixed intention of killing myself. I would look out of the window, and say good-bye to the moon and the stars, to the sleeping girls . . . and then I would go back to bed again and fall asleep."

The walk continued, so did their intimate talk. Then they went home to make the tea, a ceremony during which Hogg was always extremely funny. After tea Harriet offered to read to him, but of what she read to him that evening he retained no notion. When she said "good night" and left him, he asked himself, "Can she be good?"

When he saw her next day he told her he was madly in love with her.

Harriet was upset and indignant. For a child of sixteen, she defended herself fairly well. She spoke of Shelley and of Virtue. "Don't you see how odious your behaviour is? Percy gave me into your care and you betray his confidence. . . . But I'm sure you are cured already. . . . Please don't say another word about it. . . . And I will say nothing to Percy so as not to grieve him."

She spoke with vivacity. Love scenes are a pretty woman's battlefields and soldiers enjoy fighting. Harriet's courage was victorious, and Hogg promised to be good.

That evening, when he returned from work,

79

he saw sitting by Harriet's side on the sofa a big woman, with raven-black hair, a face of a dead white, and a horse-like profile. "Hogg, this is Eliza. She is come. Isn't it kind of her? Eliza, this is Hogg, our greatest friend, of whom Percy has so often spoken to you."

Eliza shadowed him a bow from the nape of her neck.

"I thought Bysshe was to have brought you with him?"

"Oh dear no!" said Eliza, and she went on talking to Harriet and paid him no further attention.

Hogg was not used to such treatment in the Shelleys' house.

"So this is Eliza?" he thought. "She is hideous and common-looking. Here's an end to my flirtation with Harriet—though perhaps that's just as well. . . ."

"Harriet dearest," he said aloud, "aren't we going to have any tea to-day? You don't take tea, Miss Westbrook?" he inquired, turning to her politely.

"Oh dear no!" replied that lady.

"And you, Harriet?"

"No, I won't either."

Hogg resigned himself to making his own tea, and to drinking it in silence.

From this day forth the house became insupportable. Eliza took over, or rather resumed, the management of everything. She had managed Harriet her whole life through, and though she had been obliged to relinquish her post to Shelley during the first few weeks of marriage, she now again took her place on the bridge like a captain on his ship, who runs his flag up to the mast-head, and tolerates no other authority on board.

She began by criticizing severely Shelley's conduct. "So if I hadn't come you would have been left alone with this young man? It's unbelievable! And he calls you 'dearest'? And you permit him to do so! Good heavens! What would Miss Warne say!"

When Hogg proposed a walk, "What are you thinking of?" said Eliza. "Harriet is very tired, not well at all . . ."

Hogg was astounded. "Harriet?" he repeated. "What on earth's the matter with her?"

"It's her poor nerves; you must be blind not to see it."

When Harriet wanted to read aloud to Hogg the virtuous counsels of Idomeneus, of which he stood so much in need: "Read aloud, Harriet? Whatever will become of your poor nerves? What would Miss Warne say?"

81

"Who the deuce *is* Miss Warne?" Hogg asked Harriet so soon as Eliza had gone to her room.

"She is Eliza's greatest friend, and we have the highest opinion of her."

"Why?" Is she anything extraordinary by birth and education?"

"Oh dear no, her father keeps a public-house like ours."

Hogg heaved a sigh and lifted his eyebrows.

"What does that dear Eliza do in her bed-room? Does she read?"

"No."

Harriet leaned over him to say in tones of mystery: "She brushes her hair."

"Let's go out, Harriet . . ."

At first Harriet refused, but as the hair-brushing was prolonged she agreed to accompany Hogg for a few minutes.

Since his first attempt on her virtue he had kept his promise "to be good." She was pleased —but disappointed. Quite sure of herself, she would have enjoyed temptation.

They stood on the high centre of the old Roman bridge; there was a mighty flood. The Ouse had overflowed his banks, carrying away with him timber and what not.

"Harriet dearest, think how nicely Eliza would spin down the river! How sweetly she would turn round and round like that log of wood. . . . And gracious heavens! What would Miss Warne say?"

Harriet turned away her head to hide her laughter. Hogg said dreadful things, but really he was too funny.

"You have such a delightful laugh, Harriet! . . . so musical, so gay!"

Harriet, full of courage, felt the battle was close at hand.

CHAPTER XI

HOGG (*Continued*)

SHELLEY returned next day sooner than was expected. He had had no success. His father had refused to see him. From very different motives to Shelley's, he too considered his son's marriage the unforgivable crime.

"I'd have willingly supported any amount of illegitimate children," he told Captain Pilfold. "But that he should have *married* her . . . never speak to me of him again!"

Miss Hitchener, afraid for her reputation, had refused to make the journey with Shelley. In London he learned that Eliza had not waited for him. He reached York, tired and out of spirits, hoping to find consolation in the society of his wife and his friend. What he found was an atmosphere of embarrassment and constraint.

Eliza, shut up in her room, brushed her hair all day long. Harriet and Hogg, instead of their former gay nonsense round the tea-tray, treated each other with studied coldness. When Hogg spoke to her, she replied very shortly. There was something mysterious in the air.

The moment Harriet and Shelley were alone, "Dear," he began, "I don't like this haughty attitude you take with Hogg? He is my best friend. He has looked after you in my absence. That you now have your sister with you is no reason for neglecting Hogg, whom I look on as a brother."

Harriet sighed. "He's a nice sort of friend!" said she, in a tone heavy with insinuations.

Shelley, astonished, urged her to explain.

She told the story. "He has made love to me . . . twice. The first time he told me he was passionately in love with me. . . . I pretended it was a joke. . . . I made him be quiet. I imagined it was all over, and I even had no intention of speaking to you about it. But yesterday he began again. He declared he couldn't live without me, and that he will kill himself if I don't consent."

Shelley felt his blood freeze. His heart seemed to stand still.

"Hogg? Hogg did this? But did you not point out to him . . . ?"

"Oh, I said everything I could say. . .

that he was a false friend, that he was betraying your confidence. . . . 'What does all that matter when one is in love?' he replied. 'It's all right for Percy, who is a cold and pure spirit, to talk of virtue . . . but I'm in love with you, and the rest doesn't count . . . Besides, what harm should we do Shelley? He need never know. Why not give me your love, and give him your affection? Does he think so much about you?'"

"He said that?"

"Yes, and lots of other things as well. He said you mix logic with things where it has no business, that you are a flame for ideas, and ice for the sentiments which alone count in life. . . . I answered him as well as I was able. . . ."

Shelley let himself fall upon the sofa. Suddenly the world seemed eclipsed behind a veil of grey. He was seized with giddiness, his head swam, he shivered with cold.

"That Hogg should have tried to seduce my wife, taking advantage of the moment that I had confided her to his protection . . . Hogg, on whose countenance I have sometimes gazed till I fancied the world could be reformed by gazing too . . . Never was there a more shameful attempt. . . . And yet when I think of

Oxford, of his nobility and disinterestedness,
. . . I must talk with him, I must make him
see reason. . . ."

He kissed Harriet tenderly, and begged Hogg
to walk with him to the fields beyond York.
Hogg knew there must be a scene. He was
prepared for it. He denied nothing.

"Yes, it's true. I've been in love with Harriet since the first day I saw her in Edinburgh.
Is it my fault? I can't resist beauty in women,
and Harriet is admirably beautiful. I repeat
I fell in love with her at once."

"It is not love, but lust. A low animal instinct.
Not the exalted passion which differentiates Man
from the brute. Love? Think a little, Hogg.
Love supposes self-forgetfulness, and the desire
for the happiness of the beloved object. You
could only bring about Harriet's misery. Therefore, your feelings are not those of love, but of
egotism. . . ."

"Call it what you like . . . What do words
signify? It is anyhow a terrible passion, which
I should have fought against had I not felt it
was invincible."

"No passion is invincible. Our will can
always be victorious. Had you thought of me
. . . This revelation has aged and broken me

87

more than twenty years of misery could have done . . . My heart seems seared . . . and then there is Harriet. Do you not suppose that all this has been very painful for her?"

Hogg was pale, cast-down. He looked ashamed and unhappy, and he felt so. For he too loved Shelley and he blamed his own conduct severely: "No woman in the world," he thought, "is worth the sacrifice of such a friend." Then aloud, "I'm awfully sorry, Bysshe, for what has happened. I'll try to forget, and do you and Harriet try to forgive me. Let us begin life anew as it was before. Don't be angry with me any longer. . . ."

"I'm not angry with you; I hate your crime, but not yourself. I hope that one day you will regard this horrible error with as much disgust as I do. When that day comes, you will no longer be responsible for it. The man who feels remorse is no longer the man who was guilty. It is certainly not I who would ever then reproach you, for I value a human being not for what it has been, but for what it is."

Shelley felt such satisfaction at having trodden down his anger and his jealousy, at having discovered for Hogg the way of salvation, that the offence was almost forgotten.

But women are much less indulgent. When Shelley on going home announced that he had forgiven the criminal: "What!" cried Eliza, "you mean to go on living with that fellow? Good heavens! What will become of Harriet's poor nerves?"

Hogg, coming in from his chambers next day, found an empty house.

CHAPTER XII

FIRST ENCOUNTER WITH MIDDLE AGE

SHELLEY and the two girls, in their flight from the deplorable Hogg, had decided to go to the Lakes. There was a sentimental reason for this, very like his choice of Poland Street. Two great poets, both Liberals, Southey and Coleridge, had long lived in the Lake District and by some happy chance it might be that Shelley would make their acquaintance. Nothing could have delighted him more than to meet some of the rare great minds that shared his ideas.

The Shelleys found at Keswick a small furnished cottage set in flowers. They had no right to the garden, but the landlord, who looked upon Shelley and Harriet as little better than a pair of strayed children, allowed them to run about in it.

The postman soon came to know the weight of Shelley's letter-bag. First, there was the correspondence with Hogg, which was very discouraging. He wrote long letters to Harriet in which he swore to respect her, and at the same time, to adore her during time and eternity. Such unasked-for constancy wearied her, yet her pride fed on it. When Shelley said, "Time and distance will make him forget you," she shook her head with an air of scepticism. Really sorry for the unhappiness of her admirer, she would perhaps have been more sorry to believe it could be cured: "Distance," said she, "may ease trifling griefs, but only increases great ones." When Hogg wrote, "Either Harriet must forgive me or I'll blow out my brains at her feet," she triumphed and was sad. But when no pistol-shot came to shatter their flowery solitude, she was reassured—and disappointed.

Then, there were the letters of Miss Hitchener who, since the fall of Hogg, had become Shelley's only confidant. Nearly every day he sent her a few urgent and exemplary pages. Harriet would often add to her husband's eloquent dissertations a warm invitation to come and join them.

The Duke of Norfolk lived in the neighbourhood. He had already brought about one reconciliation between Shelley and his father, and as the money question became more and more serious, they decided to write to him again.

The Duke replied by inviting Shelley, his wife, and his sister-in-law, to spend the week-end at Greystoke. He took an interest in the young man possibly through natural benevolence, possibly because it was his duty, as head of a great political party, to win the friendship of one, destined it would seem when he came of age, to go into Parliament, and to inherit £6000 a year.

Harriet, at Greystoke, bore herself with grace. The Duchess, who had been told the story of Shelley's extraordinary marriage, was agreeably surprised by the beauty and good manners of his wife. Even Eliza was considered "quite charming," at least according to Harriet. The visit was successful. When Mr. Westbrook knew that his daughters had stayed with a duke, and that his son-in-law had arrived at the castle with only a guinea in his pocket he felt the sudden need to show himself generous, and he offered the young couple an allowance of £200 a year.

Mr. Shelley could not be less open-handed, above all when his suzerain and chief asked him to be clement. He agreed once more to allow his son £200 a year: and thus all danger of poverty came to an end.

But in Percy's eyes the chief satisfaction lay

in having obtained these important results without any concessions on his part: "I think it my duty to say that however great advantages might result from such concessions I can make no promise of concealing my opinions in political or religious matters. . . . Such methods as these would be unworthy of us both." His father answered: "If I make you an allowance it is simply to prevent you from swindling strangers." So incapable was he of rising to the height of Shelley's ideas.

. . . .

At Greystoke Shelley made acquaintance with William Calvert, a friend of Southey's, who offered to take him to call on the poet. Thus, for the first time, he was to see in the flesh one of the writers he most admired. But when he actually met Southey he was intensely surprised, for he had always associated the idea of a poet with the most entrancing and aërial of beings.

What he found, in a well-furnished and well-warmed house, was a Mrs. Southey resembling far more a cook-housekeeper than a Muse. She had been in point of fact a dressmaker, and she bound her husband's books with remnants of the gowns she had made. Her linen-closets were the sanctuaries in which she exercised her talents, and her conversation was of money, cooking, and servants, like the most boring of housewives. The poet seemed insensible to the ignominy of it all. He was an honest creature, but with no reasoning powers. He admitted the social system needed changing, but declared that change could only come very slowly. He made use of the odious formula, "Neither you nor I will live to see it." He was opposed to Catholic Emancipation and Parliamentary reform. Worst of all he called himself a Christian! Grieved to the heart, Shelley left him.

Southey, worthy man, was far from imagining the impression he had made. "An extraordinary boy!" thought he, after his visitor had gone. "His chief sorrow seems to be that he is heir to an immense property, and he is as much worried by the notion that he will have £6,000 a year, as I used to be at his age by the knowledge that I hadn't a penny. Apart from this, he acts upon me as my own ghost would do. He is just what I was in 1794. He thinks himself an Atheist but is really a Pantheist: a childish ailment through which we have all passed. It is lucky he has fallen on me. He could not have a better doctor. I have prescribed Berkeley and before the week is out he will be a Berkleian. It has surprised him a good deal to meet for the
94

first time in his life with a man who perfectly understands him and does him full justice. . . . God help us! The world wants mending, though he does not set about it exactly in the right way. Yet I do not despair of convincing him that he may do a great deal of good with £6000 a year."

Thus did Youth and Middle Age meet upon their way, and the former looked at the latter with respect, but with impatience. But Middle Age looked at Youth with a kindly irony, and promised himself to dominate it by the strength of a more cultivated mind.

Middle Age forgot that the minds of different generations are as impenetrable one by the other as are the monads of Leibnitz.

Southey and his wife did all in their power to be of service to the young couple. He persuaded Shelley's landlord to reduce the weekly rent of Chestnut Cottage. Mrs. Southey gave poor Harriet, who knew nothing of housekeeping, excellent advice on cookery and laundry work. She even lent her bed- and table-linen, which was the high-water mark of favour. But a discovery which Shelley now made rendered useless every advance on the part of Middle Age.

He read by chance in a review an article by Southey in which he spoke of George III as "the best King who had ever sat upon a throne."

A blatant piece of flattery of course, but Southey aspired to be Poet Laureate, and the road to official honours is steep to climb. Shelley never pardoned baseness of this sort. He wrote to him that henceforward he should look upon him as a wage-earning slave, an upholder of crime, and he would see him no more.

And at this precise moment he troubled himself very little about Southey, for he had just discovered Godwin, the great Godwin, the author of *political Justice*, the destroyer of marriage, the enemy of the divinity, the atheist, republican and revolutionary. Godwin was still alive, he lived in London, he had a postal address like everybody else, one could send letters on Virtue to Virtue's own high prophet!

"You will be surprised," he wrote, "to receive a letter from a stranger. No introduction has authorized that which ordinary men would describe as a liberty. But it is a liberty, which if not sanctioned by custom, is far from being blamable by reason. The dearest interests of humanity demand that fashionable etiquette should not divide man from man.

"The name of Godwin has been used to excite in me feelings of reverence and admiration. I have been accustomed to consider him a luminary

too dazzling for the darkness which surrounds
him. . . . You will not, therefore, be surprised
at the inconceivable emotions with which I learnt
your existence and your dwelling. I had enrolled
your name in the list of the honourable dead.
It is not so. You still live, and I firmly believe
are still planning the welfare of human kind.

"I have but just entered on the scene of human
operations, yet my feelings and my reasonings
correspond with what yours were. My course
has been short, but eventful. . . . The ill-treat-
ment I have met with has more than ever impressed the truth of my principles on my judgment."

When Godwin received this letter he was well
pleased. Much talked of at the moment that
Political Justice appeared, he had fallen back
since into comparative neglect. He, too, though
with less reason than his young disciple, could
talk of an "eventful life." He began his career
as a clergyman, and at the age of thirty was an
avowed atheist and republican.

In 1793 he had published his famous book.
Pitt was in half a mind to have him prosecuted
for it, but the high price of the work—it was
sold at six guineas—had seemed to the Prime

Minister a sufficient protection against its dangerous teaching.

Four years later Godwin had married Mary Wollstonecraft, a woman writer of genius, with whom he had been living. She had died in giving birth to a daughter, and the inveterate enemy of marriage at once married a second time, a certain Mrs. Clairmont. This lady, who was a widow, lived in the next house to his, and had made his acquaintance by addressing gross flattery to him from her balcony.

The couple led a thorny life. There were five children, the offspring of complicated crossings. First, the daughter of Mary Wollstonecraft and Godwin, by Genius out of Genius; she was named Mary. Then two children from Mrs. Clairmont's first marriage, Jane and Charles. Thirdly, a little boy, son of Godwin and Mrs. Clairmont. Finally, the eldest in age, was a young girl who no longer belonged to anyone in the house, the daughter of Mary Wollstonecraft and her American lover, Captain Gilbert Imlay. This was the gentle and attractive Fanny Imlay, the Cinderella of the household.

The second Mrs. Godwin, "a disgusting woman who wore green spectacles," had a mendacious tongue and a nasty temper. She treated Fanny and Mary with harshness, and

98

managed the Juvenile Library in Skinner Street, which Godwin had started. The poor Philosopher led a sorrowful and difficult existence, entirely weaned from any sops to his vanity. On this account, a disciple writing him an enthusiastic letter from Keswick was extremely welcome. For a publisher of Children's Books snowed under by Bills of Exchange, nothing could be more opportune than the acquaintance of a man who considered him as a luminary too dazzling for close inspection.

He answered Shelley's letter by saying he should be glad to have a few personal details concerning his unknown correspondent. By return of post he received an autobiography, in which Timothy Shelley and the Dean of Oxford played ignoble parts. He was informed that his correspondent would inherit £6000 a year, that he was married to a woman who shared all his ideas, and that he had already published two novels and a pamphlet, all of which he was sending to "the regulator and former" of his mind.

This enthusiastic epistle was read with great excitement by the young girls of the Godwin-Clairmont household, but the author of *Political Justice* was somewhat dubious about it. Since becoming himself the father of a family, he valued paternal authority more highly than heretofore.

Possibly Mr. Timothy Shelley had only acted in his son's interests? One ought not to criticize the powers that be, when one is young, above all one ought not to publish such criticisms. While yet a scholar, one ought to have no intolerable itch to become a teacher.

Had anyone but the "venerated" Godwin written this, he would have been relegated at once to the class of stipended upholders of Intolerance. But Authority and Hierarchies are so essential to Youth, even to rebellious Youth, that it humbles itself with delight before the chosen director of its conscience.

The mystic side of Shelley's nature had more need than another's of some shrine at which to worship. "I am willing to become a scholar; nay a pupil," he replied. "My humility and confidence is unfeigned and complete, where I am conscious that I am not imposed upon, and where I perceive talents and powers so undoubtedly superior."

In his delight at having discovered Godwin, he mapped out the vastest schemes. To completely change the lives of others, to join their destiny to his own, appeared to him child's play. Hadn't he succeeded perfectly in the case of Harriet and of Eliza? What could be simpler than to hire a big house in Wales and there have Miss

Hitchener, Godwin his "venerated" friend and the whole of Godwin's charming family to live with him!

But first, being slightly stung by Godwin's scepticism, he wished to prove in a striking manner that despite his youth he knew how to act. Before settling down "for ever" in the Welsh "Home of Meditation," he would go to Ireland with Harriet and Eliza, and there spend three months working for Catholic Emancipation in particular, and the improvement of the distressful country in general.

How were the fair Harriet and Eliza of the much-brushed hair going to emancipate the Irish Catholics? The question was left unanswered, but Shelley took with him "An Address to the Irish," so full of philosophy, wise counsels, and love of humanity, that it seemed impossible the mere reading of it would not touch every heart.

Thus did the young Knight Errant of the luminous eyes take ship to conquer the Green Island. In place of a lance he carried a manuscript, the Beauteous Harriet was his lady and the Black Eliza his squire; the latter being in charge of the money, the housekeeping, and all the dirty jobs.

CARL A. RUDISILL LIBRARY
LENOIR RHYNE COLLEGE

CHAPTER XIII

SOAP BUBBLES

THE Knight of the Rueful Countenance got stoned by the galley-slaves whom he wished to free. Shelley was greeted with cat-calls when, at a meeting of the friends of Catholic Emancipation, he affirmed that it was harmful to refuse public employment to the Irish because of their religion, since one religion is as good as another. His audience much preferred the fanaticism of its persecutors to the scepticism of its defender.

The famous Address was on the same subject. It showed that Catholic Emancipation is a step on the road to total emancipation, and that morality and not expediency should be the principle of politics. Instead of expecting their freedom from the British, the Irish should free themselves by becoming sober, just, and charitable. Shelley imagined that his teaching would go straight to the heart of the poor Dubliners, and he held himself ready for martyrdom in the cause.

102

Harriet was not less enthusiastic, and her reforming ardour was a joy to behold. With pockets stuffed with pamphlets, the young couple walked up and down Sackville Street, and when they met anyone with a "likely air" they slipped a soul-saving paper into his hand; or from the balcony of their lodgings they spread sound doctrine by dropping Addresses on the heads of the passers-by. When Shelley put one adroitly into the hood of an old woman's cloak, Harriet, ready to die of laughter, was obliged to rush away. The conversion of the Irish was assuredly the most amusing of games. Godwin and Miss Hitchener expected every day to hear of Shelley's arrest. The school-teacher even considered the possibility of a political assassination. But Dublin Castle learned with composure that a young Englishman, nineteen years of age, had just made a speech on Virtue.

The police sent a copy of the Address to the Secretary of State, and Shelley's advice to the Irish on sobriety and toleration struck the official mind as a screaming joke.

Such impunity was very discouraging, nor were the ways of the Irish themselves any less so. "The reason they drink so much whisky," said kind-hearted Harriet, "is because meat is so dear." When Shelley tried to save some

wretched creature run in for theft or brawling,
the policeman, with a smile of pity, would prove
to him the man was drunk.

On St. Patrick's Night everybody was drunk,
and there was a ball at the Castle. Percy and
Harriet watched the starving people crowd round
the State carriages to admire the finery. Such
a want of dignity reduced Percy to despair.

That they themselves might set an example
of plain living, all three became vegetarians, and
Shelley thus freed himself from the remorse he
felt when thinking of the "horrors of the
slaughterhouse," and the "massacre of the bird-
innocents." They only broke the rule when
Mrs. Nugent came to dinner. She was their
sole acquaintance in Dublin, a dressmaker by
trade. It was just one of the difficulties of their
position that they knew nobody amongst these
Irish whom they loved so much. "I suppose,"
said Harriet, "that the moment Percy becomes
famous we shall know everybody all at once."

But Shelley himself hadn't much hope. In
the land of baseless and visionary fabrics where
he usually wandered, down-trodden Ireland
figured as a proud and beautiful female, Shelley
as a knight-errant and apostle, ready to fight for
her and die if need be: crowds of tatterdemalions
followed them in the streets: barbarous British

soldiers stopped him and cudgelled him: but the heroic sweetness of his gospel tamed the brutes themselves, and philosophy worked the miracle of reconciling hostile races.

Little by little this brilliant fantasy melted away, the last shred of rainbow-tinted mist floated over dirt-blackened houses, and the real Ireland loomed up, a huge solid mass of towns, farms, forests, an incalculable number of obscure and dissimilar men, a heap of immemorial traditions and laws; the land of gambling, hunting, and blood-feuds; seat of the magistrature, garrison for the soldiery, centre for the police; Ireland wretched but jeering, suffering but garrulous, discontented, and rejoicing in her discontent. The Enigmatical Island, the Absurd Island. Gazing at the terrifying Reality, what could he do? What could he hope for? He was crushed and tired out.

With growing insistence Godwin urged his disciple to give up the game. Ever since Shelley had hailed him as a spiritual father he had adopted the paternal tone, a grumbling and hostile one.

"Believe me, Shelley," he prophesied, "you are preparing a bath of blood!"

Could he have seen his spiritual son drawing up an inoffensive "Proposal for an Association for the Good of Mankind," with Eliza on one side sewing at a crimson cloak, and Harriet preparing a meal of bread and honey on the other, he might have felt more tranquil.

However, his exhortations were so far useful that they gave Shelley a decent excuse to give up rescuing the oppressed who didn't want to be rescued.

Except for a few poor creatures who knew how to sponge on him successfully, no one in Dublin took him seriously. For if in the eyes of an Irishman there is any one thing more ridiculous than an Englishman, it is an Englishman who loves Ireland, and if in the whole world there is any one spectacle which an old Eton boy and Oxford man cannot endure, it is Irish disorder and dirt.

Having seen close at hand the folly and the misery of the people, his thoughts turned with longing to the beauty and peace of the English country-side.

"I give in," he wrote to his "venerated" friend. "Never again will I address myself to the ignorant. . . . I will content myself with being the cause of an effect which will manifest itself years after I myself am dust."

Harriet packed up all the remaining pamphlets and forwarded them to Miss Hitchener, who could have very well done without this "inflammable matter."

Eliza folded up the crimson cloak, and the three apostles took the boat back to England.

.   .   .   .

The second part of their programme was now to be carried out, the house in Wales, where the "spiritual flock" could be brought together, and *all* problems solved. They thought they had found just the very thing, in the district where Shelley had stayed before his marriage. The wildness and beauty of the country attracted him. Near the house a mountain torrent brawled over the stones, and formed pools on which he had floated a little boat a foot long. His sail had been a £5 note: a terrified cat his passenger. He hoped that Miss Hitchener would persuade her father to come and farm the property of one hundred and thirty acres.

But the affair hung fire. The house was too dear. Mr. Hitchener, indignant at the Cuckfield slanders concerning Shelley and his daughter, refused to let her go to Nangtwillt. The school-teacher, proud of the invitation she had received, had very imprudently boasted of it to every one, and every one, led by Aunt Pilford, construed it in the worst possible way.

Once again was Shelley astounded by the

world's malignancy. He, who had run away
with his wife, and made a Scotch love-marriage,
how could anyone suppose he would be unfaithful
to Harriet! The idea caused him such an
overwhelming surprise that a less virtuous woman
than Miss Hitchener might have been offended
by it.

As for Mr. Hitchener, he got the treatment he
merited. He, too, was a retired public-house
keeper, for the gods seemed to delight in putting
the crystalline Shelley in connection with "the
trade." "Sir," he wrote to the lady's father,
"I have some difficulty in repressing my indignant astonishment on hearing that *you* refuse
my invitation to *your daughter*. By what right?
Who made you her master? . . . Neither the
laws of Nature nor yet those of England have
put children on the footing of personal property.
. . . Adieu. When next I hear from you I
hope that time will have liberalized your sentiments."

. . . .

As the Shelleys were going to leave Wales,
Godwin mentioned to them a most desirable
cottage which one of his friends wanted to let.
His advice was always respected. Shelley and
Harriet went to see the cottage and found it
hopeless. The house was commonplace, scarcely

finished and far too small for them. But, on their way back from this useless journey, they discovered a very picturesque village. Thirty cottages with thatched roofs covered with climbing roses and myrtles, formed the delightful hamlet of Lynmouth. By a miracle, one of the cottages was to let. It was the best situated, above a wooded gorge. From the windows you looked down upon the sea, three hundred feet below. They instantly decided to settle there "for ever."

The "venerated friend," on news of this, wrote a stiff letter. He said, harshly, that the tastes of the Shelleys were too luxurious, and that a small house, modest as it might be, ought to suffice for one who called himself Godwin's disciple. Had Timothy Shelley written such a letter the most violent epithets would have been hurled at his head, but one naturally accepts from a stranger what one would never put up with from one's own father.

Shelley did not think of complaining, but of justifying himself. If he had said that the house recommended by his guide, philosopher, and friend was too small, this was not from a wish for luxury, or even for comfort. But the number of rooms was too few, and it seemed to him hardly the thing for two persons of opposite sex and unmarried to share the same bedroom? He knew that in a regenerated society this prejudice would disappear, but in the present state of things, promiscuity appeared to him imprudent. However, he advanced this opinion —which he feared was rather reactionary—with precaution. The Master was good enough to forget it.

The adorable cottage at Lynmouth was soon the scene of a great event, the arrival of Miss Hitchener. Shelley promised himself that she would add to his life the element of intellectual collaboration, so far rather wanting to it. Nor would Harriet lose anything by the arrangement, for her "spiritual sister" would help him to form her, both young women being, he thought, sufficiently high-minded to accept these parts.

With surprise the Lynmouth villagers now saw him set off of a morning on long expeditions with this gaunt, bony stranger. And henceforth it was with her that he discussed all plans for the propagation of his ideas. The diffusion of Virtue was growing difficult. A London printer had just been sentenced to the pillory. The fate of Galileo did not frighten Shelley for himself, but he would not thrust an innocent printer into danger.

Luckily, the Magician had at his disposal

ways and means which defied the police of Lord
Castlereagh. When he had written some fine
incendiary pamphlet, he would put it in a little
box, well resined and waxed, with a lead below,
and a tiny mast and sail above, and launch it
on the ocean, or he would make small fire-
balloons, and having loaded them with Wisdom
set them sailing up into the summer sky. Or he
would watch entranced a flotilla of dark-green
bottles tightly corked, and each containing a
divine remedy, rise and sink as the emerald
waves swayed them seaward.

After he had "worked" hard in this manner,
his favourite relaxation was blowing soapbub-
bles. Seated before the door, churchwarden in
hand, he blew glassy spheres that reflected all
the forms and colours of heaven and earth upon
their tenuous surfaces. He watched them float
away until they broke and vanished.

Then quitting for a short time the aërial,
translucent palaces of Logic, he experienced the
need of fixing in verse the intangible beauty of
these shimmering violets, greens, and golds.

CHAPTER XIV

THE VENERATED FRIEND

THE roses of Lynmouth were fading, and autumn winds swept the loose clouds like dead leaves across the sky. Miss Hitchener's star was about to set. The constant presence of a stranger wearied Harriet. Shelley himself saw the dream dissolve, revealing grosser forms, and was surprised to find installed at his side a mediocre and twaddling woman. He sought his heroine in vain, and repented of his folly.

After having insisted so strenuously in dragging her from her school it was difficult to send her back there. Yet to go on living with her in an autumnal solitude was becoming unbearable. Perhaps in a big city other friends and other distractions might help him to forget the obsession of her company. At the same time, Godwin urged the Shelleys to come back to London. They resolved to go and make a long stay.

THE VENERATED FRIEND

It was with great excitement that one day in October, 1812, they left their hotel in St. James's Street to pay their first visit to Godwin and his family. Harriet, tiny, fair, and rosy, tripped by the side of her tall and round-shouldered boy-husband. They wondered what sort of welcome the Great Man was going to give them? Miss Hitchener, who had called in Skinner Street on her way through London, had met with a cold welcome. But maybe that proved nothing but the perspicacity of Godwin.

They found the whole family gathered together in the dwelling-house above the Juvenile Library, for the Godwins, on their side, were devoured with curiosity to see the Shelleys. There was the Philosopher himself, short, fat, bald, intellectual-looking, with the appearance of a Methodist parson, like almost all the theorists of Revolution.

The second Mrs. Godwin had put on her best black silk, and only wore the green glasses just for the time needed to take stock of the Baronet's grandson and his pretty wife. The Shelleys had been warned that she was a scandal-monger, but on this occasion she showed herself amiable.

Fanny Imlay was there too, gentle and pensive; and Jane Clairmont, a beautiful and vivacious brunette of the Italian type.

"The only one absent," said Godwin, "is my daughter Mary now in Scotland. She is very like her mother whose portrait I will show you."

He took the young couple into his study, and Shelley, much moved, looked long at the portrait of the fascinating Mary Wollstonecraft. Then every one sat down and Godwin and Percy talked of the relation between matter and spirit, the position of the clergy, and of German literature. The women listened in mute admiration. Harriet thought that Godwin resembled Socrates; he had the same bulgy forehead; and that Percy sitting beside him was like one of the handsome Greek youths whose ardent impatience was tempered with respect.

．　．　．　．　．　．　．

A close intimacy began between the Shelleys and the Godwins. Godwin often came round to the hotel to take Shelley for a walk, or Mrs. Godwin invited Harriet and Percy to dinner. She even invited Eliza and Miss Hitchener, but the last very unwillingly. Sometimes Harriet ventured to give a dinner herself.

On the 5th November, Guy Fawkes Day, the Shelleys dined with the Godwins. After dinner little William Godwin, aged nine, said he was

going round to let off fireworks with his friend
and neighbour, young Newton. Shelley at this
moment was discussing some profound question
or other with his venerated friend. But the
word "fireworks" instantly brought to life the
alchemist of Field Place. He hesitated just a
second between Godwin and his discourse, and
the joy of rockets and Catherine Wheels lighting
up with their many-coloured fires the old London
streets.

Then, "I'll go with you," he said to the little
boy, and off they went.

When the fireworks were over, young Newton,
enchanted by this grown-up friend who played
like a boy and could tell such wonderful stories,
took him home to introduce him to his parents.
Shelley made no resistance, and never had to
regret it. He found the Newtons adorable.
They fell at once into free, cultured and agreeable
talk.

Newton was just the man to please Shelley.
He had endless theories which he put into
practice. One of his favourite ideas was that
when Man migrated from the equatorial regions
and pushed northwards, he adopted unnatural
habits and that from these sprang all his woes.
One of such bad habits was the wearing of
clothes: Newton's children ran about the house

entirely naked. Another bad habit was the eating of flesh food; the whole Newton family was vegetarian. Nothing could arouse more surely Shelley's enthusiasm, and Mr. Newton supplied him with new arguments.

"Man has no similarity with any carnivorous animal; he is without claws to hold his prey; the formation of his teeth points out that his food should be vegetables and fruit. He first knew sickness after taking to flesh-eating, which, for him, is poison. Here you have the meaning of the story of Prometheus, which is evidently a vegetarian myth. Prometheus, that is to say Man, discovered fire and invented cooking; immediately a vulture began to gnaw at his liver. The vulture is hepatitis, that's quite clear."

Since the Newtons had taken to vegetarianism they had never needed any doctors nor any drugs. The children were the healthiest in the world, and Shelley, who had many opportunities of seeing the little girls, found them beautiful as sculptors' models.

He became a constant visitor, and the moment his voice was heard in the hall the five children rushed downstairs to meet him, and take him up with them to the nursery. Mrs. Newton and her sister Madame de Boinville were just as infatuated with him as were the children.

THE VENERATED FRIEND

At Godwin's Fanny and Jane passed whole evenings in listening to him with ecstasy. They raved of his beauty, and his arguments appeared to them unassailable. Even in a family of republicans this young aristocrat, heir to an immense fortune and so disdainful of money, shone with a romantic light.

As for him, between the two young girls, Fanny, gentle and reserved, Jane, hot-blooded and vehement, he seemed to be back again in those happy days of youthful fervour and high enthusiasm, when a bevy of adoring sisters and cousins clipt him round.

Harriet pleased the Godwin girls less. They noticed that she never thought for herself but simply repeated her husband's favourite phrases and that her grammar was faulty.

"Poor dear Shelley!" said they, so soon as the couple had left them. "He certainly has not got the wife he ought to have."

This is an impression very general amongst young women who see the man they would have liked themselves in the possession of another. They even ventured to attack Harriet, in her absence, with tiny pin-pricks; they guessed intuitively those criticisms to which her doctrinaire husband would be most sensitive.

"Harriet frightens me," wrote Fanny, "she is such a fine lady." Shelley was indignant.

"Harriet a 'fine lady'? And it is you who accuse her of this crime, in my eyes the most unforgivable of any? The ease and simplicity of her manners have always been her greatest charm, and are incompatible with the vulgar brilliancy of fashionable life. You will not convert me to your opinion, so long as I have before my eyes the living witness of its falsity."

Later on, this letter of Fanny's came back to Shelley's mind.

CHAPTER XV

MISS HITCHENER

HOGG, now fully reconciled with his family, returned to London after a year's exile at York to finish his law studies.

One evening as he sat reading in a comfortable arm-chair wrapped in a warm dressing-gown, a pot of hot tea by his side, he heard a tremendous knocking at the outer door of the house. Then this door was flung violently back against the wall, so that the whole building shook; Hogg recalled a pair of luminous eyes, a tall and stooping figure. . . .

"If Shelley were still friends with me, I should imagine . . ."

Some one rushing upstairs recalled rapid footsteps heard long ago on an Oxford staircase.

"No one but Shelley ever ran upstairs like that!"

The room-door opened, and there Shelley stood, hatless, with shirt-collar wide open, wild-looking, intellectual, always the image of some

119

heavenly spirit come down to earth by mistake.

"I got your address from your 'special pleader' fellow, and not without trouble! He took me for a swindler of some kind and didn't want to give it to me. What has become of you all this last year? . . . I've just got back from Ireland. . . . I went to preach humanity to the Irish Catholics. . . . Then we returned to Wales, a lovely country. . . . Harriet's all right . . . she expects a child. . . . Have you read Berkeley? . . . At this moment I'm reading Helvetius . . . very clever, but dry stuff. . . ."

Hogg looked at him with the admiration, affection, and irony of former days. Who but Shelley would start off to discuss Helvetius with a friend from whom he had parted on such bad terms a year back?

Shelley, full of animation and joy, walked about the room, opened books, put questions to which he never waited the answers, and seemed to have forgotten completely that Hogg had ever offended him.

He talked far into the night, and the men in the chambers next to Hogg knocked furiously on the walls to warn him that the high and piercing voice of his visitor prevented them from sleeping.

Hogg, alarmed for his good name, suggested

Shelley should go. Shelley continued to talk. He explained that he had just opened a subscription list to finish a dyke which would enable the Welsh at Tremadoc to regain 5000 acres of land from the sea He had headed the list with £100 and he was devoting his life, his strength, and his fortune to the enterprise. . . . Hogg, taking him gently by the arm, led him to the door, but he resisted.

"Your neighbours bore me! They are brutes who don't understand that it is only during the night that the soul feels really free."

Hogg had managed to get him out upon the landing.

"I'll go, but on one condition, and that is that you come and dine with us to-morrow. Harriet will be delighted to see you. I apologize for having a horrible creature with us, Miss Hitchener . . . but she will be leaving in a day or two."

"Miss Hitchener? The sister of your soul?"

"*She* the sister of my soul?" cried Shelley. "She's a crawling and contemptible worm. . . . We call her the Brown Demon."

But they had now reached the street. Hogg gently pushed his friend out of the house and closed the door behind him.

Next day at six o'clock, Hogg sent in his name to Harriet. She received him with enthusiasm. She looked younger, more blooming, and lovelier than ever.

"What a separation this has been!" she said. "But it will not happen again. We are now going to live in London for ever!"

Eliza sat apart in haughty silence. She gave Hogg a limp hand, without condescending to speak to him.

"You're looking delightfully well, Harriet."

"She? Oh no, poor dear thing!" said Eliza in a lackadaisical voice. "Most dreadfully shattered!"

Hogg thought, "Nothing is changed in this house; one must take care what one says."

Shelley at this moment burst into the room like a cannon ball, and dinner was brought up.

After dinner, there were mysterious whisperings from Eliza into Harriet's ear, who came obediently to bid Hogg good night, and to invite him to come again on Sunday morning.

"It's the day the Brown Demon is going, conversation will be so difficult. But you are always such good fun, you would be the greatest help to us. . . . Percy has told you about our Tormentor?"

122

At the mention of Miss Hitchener's name Eliza exhibited a deep but silent disgust.

"She's a horrible woman," Harriet went on. "She tried to make Percy fall in love with her. She pretended that he did really love her, and that I was only good for the housekeeping. Percy has promised her £100 a year if only she will go."

Shelley confirmed this. He saw the imprudence of thus sacrificing a quarter of his income, but it was necessary. The young woman had lost her situation through them, and her reputation and health into the bargain, she added, thanks to their barbarous conduct.

"She is really a horrible creature!" he said, shuddering. "A superficial, ugly, hermaphroditical beast of a woman. I've never been so astonished at my bad taste as after spending four months with her. . . . How would Hell be, if such a woman were in Heaven? And she writes poetry! She has written an Elegy on the Rights of Woman, which begins:

All, all are men, the woman like the rest. . . ."

He burst into one of his wild shouts of laughter.

Next day Hogg did not fail to turn up. The

Heroine of the day appeared to him boring but inoffensive. She was a big, bony, masculine woman, dark-skinned, and with traces of a beard.

Shelley presently declared he must go out; Harriet had a bad headache and needed quiet; Hogg's fate was to take the two Elizas for a walk.

With the Brown Demon on his right arm, and the Black Diamond, as he nicknamed Eliza Westbrook, on his left, he directed their steps towards St. James's Park. "I could say, like Cornelia: 'These are my jewels!'" he thought.

The two fair rivals attacked each other across him in phrases of haughty contempt. The languishing Eliza woke up to deal formidable blows with a calm soft acrimony. Miss Hitchener made a show of speaking only to Hogg. She discoursed on the Rights of Woman. Eliza, who could not talk on this subject, nor on any other, found herself reduced to ignominious silence.

When they got home she penned Hogg into a corner of the hall.

"How could you talk to that nasty creature so much? How could you permit her to prate so long to you? Harriet will be seriously displeased with you, I assure you! She will be very angry."

But Harriet merely smiled up at him and

asked, "Were you not tired of the Brown Demon?"

When luncheon was over he wickedly led the conversation back to Woman's Rights, and the Goddess of Reason was at once let loose. Shelley rose from his chair, came and stood before her, and fell into animated discussion. The sisters Westbrook looked at him with sorrowful dismay as at one guilty of communication with the enemy.

Eliza whispered to Hogg, "If you only knew how dirty she is you wouldn't go near her!"

But the moment of release came when the exile's bags and boxes were piled into a hackney-coach, and the women of Shelley's household were left dancing and singing for joy.

CHAPTER XVI

HARRIET

THE few months which followed the departure of Miss Hitchener were happy months. The Shelleys were still penniless wanderers, but an immense interior satisfaction replaced for them money and home. He had begun a long poem, *Queen Mab*, and to work at it made life worth living. Harriet, who was with child, was sunk in an agreeable torpor, reserving all her strength for creative purposes, and so amused by and interested in her own sensations and hopes, as to be quite insensible to boredom.

During this period they made short visits to Wales, and returned a second time to Ireland, but no longer dabbled in politics. To please Percy, Harriet began to learn Latin. He taught her on a method of his own. Discarding grammars he plunged her straight into Horace and Virgil.

While she studied, he went on with his poem or read history. Godwin had assured him that his ignorance of history was one great cause of his errors of judgment, and though he loathed the subject he set at it courageously. In the evening Harriet sang old Irish songs, "Robin Adair," and "Kate of Kearney," or they read the newspapers together, which at that time were filled with accounts of the prosecutions of Liberal writers.

Often to these persons, condemned for their opinions, Shelley would write offering to pay their fines, although they were utterly unknown to him. And, never having ten pounds in hand, he would be obliged to borrow at 400 per cent, in order to pay these fines.

Presently, it was necessary to go back to London as Harriet's time was near. Shelley was also approaching his twenty-first birthday, an important date for him, for it seemed possible he might then come to terms with his father.

They took rooms at Cooke's Hotel in Albemarle Street. Eliza, who was with them, looked after Harriet with exaggerated care. Her fussiness annoyed Shelley always in favour of letting Nature have her way. When he was absent Eliza would prime her sister in matrimonial strategy.

"It's most extraordinary that at twenty-one years of age Percy can't find a way of making up with his father, so that you could be received by the family, and lead the proper sort of life for a future baronet's wife! If you were a little more skilful and persuasive with him, things would be very different, I'm sure! You ought to have a town house of your own, your own silver, your own carriage; and all that could easily be had if Percy chose."

Harriet was of the same mind. She was a pretty woman and she knew it, and for a pretty woman a life without luxury is as hard to bear as a subordinate position for a clever man. The street admiration she meets with tells her of her power, and she knows too that youth's a stuff that won't endure. Just as a strongly armed nation desires to ensure her place in the sun, before demobilizing, Woman wishes to exact good terms for her enemy, Man, before resigning herself to the pacifism of old age.

Besides which Eliza was continually pitying Harriet, and self-pity comes so naturally to all of us, that the most solid happiness can be shaken by the compassion of a fool.

Moved thereunto by Harriet at the instigation of Eliza, and also by renewed counsel from the Duke of Norfolk, Shelley decided to write again to his father. He would not have taken this step had he not judged it to be both honourable and necessary. He desired earnestly to see his mother, and even the Squire seen from a distance of time and place appeared to him a pathetic and inoffensive figure.

"MY DEAR FATHER,

"I once more presume to address you to state to you my sincere desire of being considered as worthy of a restoration to the intercourse with yourself and my family which I have forfeited by my follies. . . . I hope the time is approaching when we shall consider each other as father and son with more confidence than ever, and that I shall no longer be a cause of disunion to the happiness of my family. I was happy to hear from John Grove, who dined with us yesterday, that you continue in good health. My wife unites with me in respectful regards."

Unfortunately Timothy Shelley, with characteristic wrong-headedness, chose a test of Bysshe's obedience to which it was impossible for him to submit; he could not write to the authorities of University College that he was now a sincere and dutiful son of the Church. And, failing this, his father declined all further communication with him.

"I am not so degraded and miserable a slave," wrote Shelley to the Duke of Norfolk, "as publicly to disavow an opinion which I believe to be true. Every man of common sense must plainly see that a sudden renunciation of sentiments seriously taken up is as unfortunate a test of intellectual uprightness as can possibly be devised. . . . I am willing to concede everything that is reasonable, anything that does not involve a compromise of that self-esteem without which life would be a burden and a disgrace."

Eliza considered such obduracy absurd. "Thus Harriet, so soon to be brought to bed, will not even have a carriage to save her running about the streets on foot!" Shelley, exasperated, bought a carriage on credit, and refused to use it. He hated being shut up in a closed carriage, and much preferred long tramps with Hogg on foot.

Though sick to death of Eliza at home, there were plenty of pleasant houses where he could take refuge. There was the Godwins' in Skinner Street, where Fanny and Jane Clairmont always received him with open arms. There was the Newtons' in Chester Square, where he found affection, intelligence, and old-world courtesy. Mrs. Newton, a first-rate musician, the favourite pupil of Dussek, would sit down to the piano, while Shelley seated on the rug amidst the children would tell them tales of ghosts and phantoms in a low voice.

Very often Madame de Boinville was on a visit to her sister. These two ladies, daughters of a wealthy St. Vincent planter, had received a mixed Anglo-French education that Shelley, tremendous admirer of the French philosophers, much appreciated. Madame de Boinville, in particular, charmed him. Her romantic marriage with a ruined *émigré,* a friend of Andre Chénier and of La Fayette, invested her with a poetic fascination. She was a woman with white hair, but with so childlike a face, such speaking eyes, a mind so lively and up-to-date, that one had more pleasure in talking with her than with many a younger woman. For the first time in his life Shelley found, in her and her sister, women whose intellectuality was on a par with his own.

The conversation of Eliza and Miss Hitchener now appeared to him thoroughly despicable.

From living with Harriet, he had fallen into the habit of looking on women as children, for whom an abstract idea must be reduced to its simplest expression. With Madame de Boinville he was astonished to find that he could not only tell her all his ideas, but that by the charm and precision of her language she gave them a new attraction. For her and her sister, as for Shelley himself, the play of thought was the finest of pastimes. Learning is nothing without cultivated manners, but when the two are combined in a woman you have one of the most exquisite products of civilization.

With a secret joy and a delicious feeling of attained perfection, Shelley realized that he had at last found surroundings propitious to his happiness, and that everything he had previously known was grotesquely unworthy of him.

The ladies, on their side, were enchanted by their discovery of Shelley, for this very good-looking and well-born young man loved ideas as they did and expressed them with warmth. He had got rid of the rather intolerant dogmatism of his sixteen years, and now in discussion showed modesty and forbearance. Never had they met a man so selfless, so generous, so above the material things of life as he. Generally serious, he yet was capable of fun, and he had the ease of manner, the contempt for ceremony, and the perfect politeness, which is the hall-mark of the young aristocrat. "What more charming," they asked themselves, "than a saint who is at the same time a man of the world?"

With a tinge of jealousy, but also with affectionate interest, Hogg watched the manœuvrings of all these pretty women round his ingenuous friend. At the Godwins', the girls called Shelley the Elf-King or the King of Faery; at the Newtons', he was known as Ariel and Oberon. The moment he appeared the women gathered about him. But he was a Spirit difficult to call up at any fixed hour. He was subject to strange caprices, sudden frights, panic terrors. Sometimes falling into a poetic vision, he forgot that he was expected at a tea-party. At other times, when he was actually caught and supposedly held fast, all at once some imaginary duty called him one knew not where.

"In certain countries," Hogg told him, "it is believed that goats, which are children of the devil, pass one hour out of every twenty-four in hell. I think you're like the goats, Shelley."

On the other hand, when engaged with a woman after his own heart in one of the serious and animated talks which he so much enjoyed, he forgot both time and place. The night waned, and Adonis still led his rather breathless priestesses conversationally onwards. Dawn broke; he was talking still. Then, as it was too late to go to bed, a walk in the delicious morning air rounded things off.

"What the devil were you talking about all

133

night to your circle of beauties?" the puzzled Hogg would inquire.

"I'm sure I don't know."

Harriet also wondered what her husband could have to say to all these women. She was now near her term, and seldom went out of doors. Shelley often left her alone. In the houses where he was a favourite, she felt that she was unwelcome. At the Godwins' she could not get on with Mrs. Godwin. At the Boinvilles' she had been thought at first charming because she was so pretty and the wife of a poet, but she was soon set down as a very ordinary woman.

CHAPTER XVII

COMPARISONS

THE child was a girl, fair, with blue eyes. Her father named her Ianthe. Her mother added Elizabeth. Thus Ovid and Miss Westbrook clasped hands over the cradle. Shelley walked about with the baby in his arms singing to it a monotonous tune of his own making. The idea of bringing up a new being that he might save from prejudices was delightful to him. As an admirer of Rousseau he expected Harriet to suckle the child herself and he was eager to give the tenderest care to both. In the excitement of his new rôle, the odious Eliza was forgotten.

But Harriet, egged on by her sister, refused to nurse the child. She engaged a wet nurse, "a hireling," as Shelley declared resentfully. But on this point Harriet was gently but firmly obstinate.

A curious change came over her after Ianthe's birth. It seemed as though she wished to make

135

up for nine months' inactivity. Her Latin lessons were not resumed. She wanted nothing now but to be out of doors looking into the bonnet-shops and jewellers' windows. To find pleasure in such idle trifling seemed to Shelley monstrous and unintelligible. He was willing to pay for any of Harriet's "reasonable" fancies, even at the price of loans and endless annoyances, but to spend the money so necessary to "persecuted writers" and other just causes, on mere "glad rags," appeared to him scandalous, and he made his wife and sister-in-law feel it.

Eliza was careful to show up Shelley's feelings.

"Percy finds money enough to pay the debts of his dear Godwin, who plucks him and whose wife is rude to us. He finds money to pay the fines for a set of miserable scribblers, but he can't afford to dress his own wife decently! He's a fool if he thinks it odd that a young and pretty woman should like bonnets. If you don't dress now at eighteen, when *can* you do so?"

Miss Westbrook encouraged at the house the visits of an army man, a certain Major Ryan, whom they had first met in Ireland, and now found again in London. He, too, was of opinion that so charming a young woman as Harriet ought to lead a more normal life. Harriet was inclined to agree with him. Latin and philosophy had really been a great strain on her. She had borne it without complaint because of her love and admiration for Percy. But shopping and gay chatter were just as much to her taste as were the Newtons to Shelley's, and the pleasure she found in these frivolities contrasted with the rather painful attention she had given to her "lessons."

Shelley thought that town life and its temptations was the cause of the trouble, and he had the very natural idea of all lovers who feel a shadow falling between them, to go back to those scenes where their love had been unclouded. Harriet's famous carriage was got ready. Shelley raised £500 by a post obit bond for £2000, and accompanied by the inevitable Eliza, went on pilgrimage to Keswick and Edinburgh.

The constant change of scene on the journey made them forget their worries, and they returned to London in much better spirits, but they had hardly settled down again when the old disagreements were renewed. Harriet and Eliza pined for a fine house, fashionable life, gowns, and a social circle. Shelley detested all these things, but detested still more the idea that his wife wanted them. He still loved her, but he began to feel a touch of contempt.

Hogg came to see them. He found Harriet

quite recovered, prettier and more blooming than
ever. But she no longer offered to read to him
the wise counsels of Idomeneus. She asked him
instead to go with her to her milliner's. She
vanished into the shop, leaving him waiting on
the pavement. She began to bore him, and as a
man has little indulgence towards the woman who
has rejected his advances, he let Shelley see it.
Shelley, too, could no longer hide his impatience.
The Shelleys had reached the dangerous moment
of confidences with a third person.

.   .   .   .

When Madame de Boinville invited Shelley
and Hogg to pass a few days with her in the
country, they accepted with joy. They found
there her daughter Cornelia, who was cultured,
pensive and pretty, and her sister Mrs. Newton.
Shelley again knew the delightful sensations of
former evenings passed with them in town. He
called Madame de Boinville, Maimouna, because
she reminded him of the heroine of *Thalaba*
whose

> . . . face was as a damsel's face
> And yet her hair was grey.

The attractive Cornelia gave the two young
men lessons in Italian, and Madame de Boinville
expounded in her delicious voice the indulgent
138

teaching of the French philosophers. "To enjoy life, and help others to enjoy it, without harming anyone, herein lies the whole of morality." This dictum of Chamfort's, which was a great favourite of Madame de Boinville, ought by rights to have roused Shelley's wrath. Poor Harriet had never said anything so flatly opposed to virtue. . . . But then she would have said it much less well.

At Bracknell even fooling seemed pleasant to Shelley, because there, the simplest games were imbued with the cast of thought. Cornelia had the habit, when she first woke up, of reading over and often learning by heart one of Petrarch's sonnets. This sonnet she thought over and fed upon all day long. When they said good morning to her, Shelley and Hogg would inquire which the day's sonnet might be. Sometimes the poem was so moving she did not trust herself to recite it, but opened the little pocket-Petrarch always carried with her, and pointed out the passage.

Walking between the two young men in the garden, she would comment on the love text with eloquence and simplicity.

"It is so good to begin the day," she said, "with a draught of tenderness which sweetens all our thoughts, words, and deeds until the night."

These walks, these talks, seemed to Shelley the only things of any real importance. The house, fine yet simple, charmed him by its perfection and the absence of the luxury which disgusted him so much. It was for him a place of repose and of freedom from care. Harriet was invited to join them. Madame de Boinville received her with kindness. "She's a very pretty little creature," she told Hogg. "But she seems to me a rather frivolous companion for our dear, delightful Stoic. However, she's not yet eighteen, I think?"

Harriet, unfortunately, saw quite well that she was not treated on a footing of equality. She saw that Percy took far more pleasure in reading Petrarch with Cornelia than in discussing with his wife how to improve their style of living; and by a reaction against an environment which she dimly felt to be hostile to her in spite of an appearance of cordiality, she put on cold and ironical airs.

When the rest of the party were solemnly debating on Virtue, or the Reform Bill, Shelley saw her exchange mocking smiles with Hogg and Peacock, a new and very sceptical friend they had just discovered.

He could forgive Hogg's irony. His wife's irritated him. Hogg's mind was an entirely different world from his, and he permitted the difference. But Harriet's mind was his very own handiwork. He had formed it, trained it, cultivated it. He was accustomed to think of it as his echo. On suddenly discovering that this other self had detached itself from him, and could sometimes even make fun of what he said, he was surprised and profoundly hurt.

There is nothing which makes a woman appear stupider than secret jealousy. Instead of attacking the foe openly, which would be natural and pathetic, she criticizes with spite innocent words and inoffensive actions, and showing a terrible want of tact gives an air of meanness to a sentiment which is perfectly justifiable. Harriet found fault with everything at Bracknell because she had good cause to be jealous of Cornelia Turner. But Shelley, who put down her scornful looks and her mocking remarks to an incredible childishness, treated her with cool contempt.

At this her pride was up in arms, and her behaviour became worse. "Eliza is right," she thought, "Percy is absolutely selfish, and thinks everything he does is perfect. Because he likes this dull life, these silly discussions, and this Italian poetry, he wants to force me to like them too. But what right has he to prevent me from living *my* life? How is Cornelia Turner reading

141

Petrarch so superior to me? These women whom he admires are neither so young nor so good-looking as I. He would very soon want me back."

With this idea in her head she announced her intention of returning to London to join Eliza. Her hostesses did nothing to dissuade her, beyond the few words of regret which politeness required. "Poor Shelley," these ladies remarked, just as the Godwin girls had done, "he has not got the wife he ought to have."

Harriet fell into the way of going up to stay with Eliza for weeks at a time, leaving her husband alone at Bracknell. Soon the usual "kind friend" let Shelley know that his wife was going about with Major Ryan. For the first time since his marriage the idea of a possible infidelity occurred to him. It was a question which in the abstract he had always treated with the greatest contempt. Suddenly brought up against it with Harriet and himself as possible actors, he was overwhelmed with the most violent grief he had yet known.

Reason told him he ought to consider himself lucky if he were freed from a very ordinary woman. If at that moment he loved at all, was it not rather the heavenly Cornelia than Harriet whose miserable spite had recently annoyed him so much? And, if he no longer loved her, to break with her would be best. He had always taught that, when passion's trance is over-past, each should be free again. But it was in vain that he reasoned thus with himself. He discovered with stupefaction that Percy Shelley and Harriet Westbrook were no longer two separate and free beings. The sum of past memories, caresses, joys, and sufferings, enmeshed them both in a web from which there was no escape.

He rushed up to town, determined either to offer Harriet his excuses or to confess his faults. But she received him with harshness and irony. Any heart-to-heart talk was out of the question.

His child-wife, so gentle and submissive only three months ago, now showed herself cold and haughty. How had such a change come about? There were instants when Shelley thought he detected beneath pride's hard surface, a fleeting image of the other Harriet, but when he sought to hold it by a loving word, it was gone. Against the steely armour of her heart he knocked in vain.

Wandering about the streets without any object, he thought: "What a fool I have been! Here I am tied for ever to a woman who does not love me, who has never loved me. Evidently

she only married me for the money and title.
. . . Now that she sees her hopes upset, she punishes me for her mistake. . . ." And he repeated
with disgust: "A heart of ice . . . a lump of ice!"

Perhaps had he ever seen her alone he would
have succeeded in thawing it, but Eliza, prim,
hostile, formidable, stood always between them,
and the gallant Major Ryan was in the wings,
ready to commiserate the cruelties of a doctrinaire husband.

After struggling for a few days, Shelley's
ardour was suddenly quenched. Capable by fits
and starts of an energy when nothing was impossible to him, he fell, as formerly after his long
tramps at Oxford, into an insurmountable torpor,
and his will-power like a dying candle-flame
threw up a final blaze of light before it expired.

When he saw that Harriet was obdurate, he
gave up all hope of saving the remnants of his
married happiness, and he wrote to Bracknell
to announce he was coming on a month's visit,
and coming alone. He knew well that after a
month's interval he would find Harriet completely ruined by her hateful surroundings, he
knew that a catastrophe would be the result of
the Bracknell interlude, but he was too tired to
carry on the fight.

"What more am I now but an insect warming

itself in a ray of sunshine? The next cloud that passes will plunge me into the frozen darkness of death." And, in melancholy mood, he recited the lines from Burns:

> But pleasures are like poppies spread,
> You seize the flow'r, its bloom is shed;
> Or like the snow-fall in the river,
> A moment white, then melts for ever.

It seemed to him that into the translucent domes of crystal wherein his fancy dwelt, Harriet, Ianthe, and Elizabeth had been suddenly flung like so many blocks of living and rebellious matter. In vain did he try with all the forces of logic to drag them out. His feeble weapons were crushed beneath the ponderous reality.

CHAPTER XVIII

SECOND INCARNATION OF THE GODDESS

THERE were days when Shelley, recalling the sweet and childlike face of his eighteen-year-old wife, thought it might still be possible to forget and make up. In a pathetic poem he tried to tell her how miserable it was for one who had lived in the warm sunshine of her eyes to die beneath her scorn. Did the lines move her? He never knew. She shut herself up more and more in feelings of pride and revenge. He had left her on several occasions. No doubt it was as a reprisal that the moment he came back to London she set off with Ianthe for Bath.

Shelley was obliged to remain in town. He had come of age, yet his affairs were no further advanced thereby. His solicitor gave him to understand there might be a family law-suit to deprive him of his rights. Although crippled with debts himself, he persisted in trying to free others from theirs. The Juvenile Library founded by Godwin had been a failure, and the
146

sight of this old fighter for justice, impoverished and saddened by money troubles, was inexpressibly painful to his young disciple and friend.

But three thousand pounds were needed to save Godwin, a big sum. Yet from the moment he knew of Shelley's wish to save him, he again exhibited great friendliness, and as Shelley was now a "bachelor" in London, his "beauteous half" being in the country for an indefinite period, he was invited to dine in Skinner Street every night.

He accepted all the more readily because he wished to see the girls again, and Godwin had informed him he would find an extra one, Mary, who had at length come home from Scotland. He gave an attractive portrait of her; seventeen years old, quick and lively, a great wish to learn, and immense perseverance. Already Fanny and Jane had described her to Shelley as being as intelligent as she was beautiful. For her mother, Mary Wollstonecraft, Shelley had the warmest admiration. He was greatly moved at the thought he was about to meet her unknown daughter.

He needed for his happiness to embody in the form of a beautiful woman the mysterious and benevolent Forces which he imagined as scattered throughout the Universe. Love was, for him, an

147

impassioned admiration, an integral act of faith, an exquisite and perfect mixture of the sensuous and the intellectual.

Had Mary not appeared at that juncture, or had she proved a disappointment, the sentiment which hovered and hesitated in his wounded heart would have dedicated itself to Fanny or to Jane, but Mary came, and his fate was settled.

Her face was very pale and pure, her golden hair arranged in smooth bands on either side of a shapely head, she had a great slab of a forehead, and earnest hazel eyes. An air of sensibility and mournful courage instantly inspired in Shelley the same enthusiasm that he found in reading Homer or Plutarch. He saw something heroic in this delicate young girl, and the mixture of the heroic and the feminine was ever that which most appealed to him.

"What seriousness and what feeling!" thought he, listening with ecstasy to her young fresh voice. A maiden standing where brook and river meet, having the grace of the woman and the intellectual eagerness of the youth, had always seemed to him one of the most exquisite works of art. He longed to put a brotherly arm round those slender shoulders, and to make those questioning eyes sparkle, as he bore her away on some astonishing gallop through the realms of aërial metaphysics.

Harriet Westbrook had only imperfectly realized his ideal. For a moment he had hoped to find in her the delightful blend of beauty and intelligence that he would so greatly have loved, but poor Harriet had not withstood the difficult test of time. She was wanting in any real brainpower; even when she had the air of being interested in ideas, her indifference was proved by the blankness of her gaze. Worst of all, she was coquettish, frivolous, versed in the tricks and wiles of woman, and this alone was sufficient to chill him to the marrow.

But Mary, of the nut-brown eyes, was slim and true as a Toledo blade. Brought up by the author of *Political Justice,* her mind appeared free from all feminine superstition; and the clear if rather piercing tones of her voice emphasized delightfully its cultivated precision. Dining every evening in the little house in Skinner Street, Shelley passed the time in looking at Mary, while he seemed to listen to Godwin who explained the regrettable state of his own affairs, and discussed the Budget, or the laws of the Press.

Mary, on her side, was quite ready to fall in love with Shelley. The romance had been prepared by the sisters, who for a month previously had talked of nothing in their letters but the handsome poet. Yet no description of Shelley ever came up to the reality.

Mary saw, at once, how much she interested him. Although he had made no complaint of life—he never did—she realized he was unhappy, and so one evening when they found themselves alone in the room where her mother's portrait hung she spoke to him of her own troubles. She adored her father, but detested Mrs. Godwin on whose account the home in Skinner Street was become odious to her. The only place in the world where she felt herself at peace was by her mother's tomb in the churchyard of old St. Pancras. She went there book in hand every fine day to read and meditate. Shelley, thrilled, asked if he might go with her.

.　　.　　.　　.　　.　　.　　.

Thus, after an interval of five years, he found himself sitting again at a young girl's side in a graveyard, but this time his companion was of a serious and impassioned soul. For the second time the Word was made Woman. But, alas, Shelley was no longer free. He felt himself drawn to Mary by an irresistible force. He longed to take her hand, to press his lips to her delicately curved ones, he knew that she desired him, as he did her, and they dared not let their eyes meet. What could he offer her? He was a married man. It is true that marriage is only a convention. When one loves no longer, one is free. He had never promised Harriet more than this; besides, believing her to be the mistress of Major Ryan, he felt no scruples on her account. But his marriage was legally indissoluble. He had nothing to offer Mary but that reprobate existence which he had not dared to impose on Harriet.

Nevertheless, a love shared, even though hopeless, is better than uncertainty and moral isolation. He determined to tell Mary the whole truth about his wife. Married love, even as it dies, long holds out behind a mask of silence against the world's assaults, but there comes a moment when a man finds a bitter joy in laying bare his wounds.

Shelley drew a picture of Harriet as he now saw her, and by an unconscious change of values lent, to his very human deception, motives of a spiritual order. He had needed a companion who could appreciate poetry and understand philosophy. Harriet was incapable of either. He took a painful pleasure, also very human, in depreciating the grapes which he had lost.

He gave Mary a copy of *Queen Mab*. Under the printed dedication of that poem to Harriet, he wrote the words, "Count Slobendorf was about to marry a woman who, attracted solely by his fortune, proved her selfishness by deserting him in prison." Back in her own room, Mary added, "This book is sacred to me, and as no other creature shall ever look into it, I may write in it what I please—yet what shall I write?—that I love the author beyond all powers of expression and that I am parted from him, dearest and only love—by that love we have promised to each other although I may not be yours, I can never be another's. But I am thine, exclusively thine.

> By the kiss of love, the glance none saw beside,
>   The smile none else might understand,
> The whispered thought of hearts allied,
>   The pressure of the thrilling hand.

I have pledged myself to thee and sacred is the gift."

Meanwhile, these glances and smiles that none might see nor understand, had been seen and perfectly understood by Godwin. The intrigue of his daughter with a married man troubled him. He pointed out the danger to her, and wrote to Shelley in the same strain. He advised him to make things up with his wife: and he begged him to discontinue, for the present, his visits to Skinner Street.

The prohibition, kindly as it was, simply hastened on events which, without it, might have tarried. Shelley, passionately in love with Mary and deprived of her society, determined to take a decisive step. He felt no remorse on Harriet's account, for he persisted in thinking her guilty, in spite of the assertions of Peacock and Hogg, both impartial witnesses. "There's just one thing only she cares about," he thought, "and that is money. I'll provide for her future, and then she'll be glad to be free." Accordingly he wrote to her begging her to come to London. She came; she was four months gone with child, and very unwell. When, calmly and kindly, Percy told her he was going to live without her and elope with some one else, but that he would remain her best friend, the shock brought on an alarming illness.

Shelley nursed her with devotion, which made her more unhappy still, and the moment she was better he resumed his inflexible arguments. "The union of the sexes is sacred only so long as it contributes to the happiness of husband and wife, and it is dissolved automatically from the moment that its evils exceed its benefits. Constancy has nothing virtuous in itself; on the contrary

153

it is often vicious, leading one to condone the
gravest faults in the object of one's choice."

When he wove round her these diaphanous
but insuperable webs, Harriet knew she was lost,
just as formerly when she had tried to defend her
religious beliefs against him she had seen herself
overwhelmed on every side. She knew that some
answer *must* exist; that so much anguish and sorrow and horror should find some expression, and
might have found it had her mind been clearer;
as it was she never knew what she ought to say.
She dreamed she was struggling to free herself
from invisible bonds. Her one relief was in terrible outbursts of rage against Mary. It was she
who was the cause of all, she who had separated
Percy from his wife, taking advantage of his
romantic tendencies to entice him to meet her at a
graveside, which was just the kind of thing that
would appeal to him. She had made a shameful
use of her mother's memory.

Mary, on her side, had not the slightest pity
for Harriet. She had formed an odious conception of her. A woman who, having had the
felicity of marrying Shelley, had yet been incapable of making him happy, could only be selfish, futile, second-rate. She knew that he would
treat Harriet with generosity, that he was going
to give an order to his banker to pay over to her

the greater part of his allowance, and this knowledge quieted her conscience. "She'll have the money, and that's all she cares about," Mary said with disdain.

Shelley was in a condition of extreme nervous agitation. All sorts of contrary sentiments warred in his soul. When he saw Harriet fall into heart-breaking fits of despair, he could not forget the delicious moments passed with her long ago, but he had only to be again in Mary's presence to consecrate himself anew to her tranquil charm.

To calm his mind he began to take laudanum as he had formerly done, but now in stronger doses. He showed the bottle to Peacock, and said: "I never part from this." He added, "I am always repeating to myself your lines from Sophocles:

> Man's happiest lot is not to be;
> And when we tread life's thorny steep,
> Most blest are they who earliest free
> Descend to death's eternal sleep."

SECOND PART

ARIEL: Was't well done?
PROSPERO: Bravely, my diligence. Thou shalt be free.

CHAPTER XIX

A SIX WEEKS' TOUR

THE post-chaise was ordered for four o'clock in the morning. Shelley waited up all night opposite Godwin's house. At length he saw the stars and the oil-lamps grow pale. Mary noiselessly opened the hall door. Jane Clairmont, who at the last moment had decided to go with her sister, looked after the luggage with zeal.

The long carriage journey greatly tired Mary, but Shelley dared not stop lest Godwin were pursuing them. At about four in the afternoon they reached Dover where, after the usual difficulties with custom-house officials, and sailors, they found a small boat which agreed to take them over to Calais.

The weather was fine. The white cliffs of England slowly faded away. The fugitives were safe. Presently the wind rose and freshened into a gale. Mary, very ill, passed the night lying upon Shelley's knees, who, himself worn

159

out with fatigue, supported her head on his
shoulder. The moon sank to a stormy horizon;
then, in total darkness, a thunderstorm struck
the sail, and the fast-flashing lightning revealed
a dark and swollen sea. When morning broke
the storm passed, the wind changed, and the sun
rose broad, and red, and cloudless, over France.

Mary shook off her somnolence in the streets
of Calais; the gay bustle of the harbour, the picturesque costume of the fisherfolk, the confused
buzz of voices speaking a strange language, re-
vived her. The day was spent at the inn, as they
had to wait for the luggage coming by the Dover
Packet, but when this arrived it brought also
Mrs. Godwin and her green spectacles. The fat
lady hoped to persuade Jane, at least, to go back
with her to Skinner Street, but Shelley's eloquence won the day, and Mrs. Godwin returned
alone. At six o'clock the travellers left Calais
for Boulogne in a cabriolet drawn by three horses
running abreast.

. . . .

Their plan was to get to Switzerland, but after
a few days in Paris their purse was empty. Shelley had a letter for a certain Tavernier, a French
man of business, who was to act as banker for
them. They invited him to lunch at the hotel,
and put him down as a perfect idiot, for he
160

seemed to have a difficulty in understanding the
absolute necessity of this journey by two little
girls and a tall and excitable young man.

Shelley had to pawn his watch and chain; he
got eight napoleons for them. This would give
them bread and cheese for a fortnight, so with
minds at ease, they began to explore the Boule-
vards, the Louvre, and Notre Dame. Later on
they preferred to remain in the hotel and re-read
together the works of Mary Wollstonecraft and
Byron's poems.

At the end of the week, Tavernier, a good
fellow in the main, agreed to lend them sixty
pounds. But, as this was not enough to pay for
their places by diligence, they decided to start
on foot, and to buy an ass to carry the luggage,
and each of them ride it by turns.

Shelley went to the cattle-market and came
back to the hotel with a very small donkey. Next
morning a hackney-coach took them to the Bar-
rier of Charenton, the ass trotting behind the
carriage.

The roads in France in the year 1814 were not
particularly safe. The armies had just been
demobilized, and bands of marauders robbed
those who travelled on them. The peasants
working in the fields by the roadside stared with
all their eyes at this extraordinary caravan of

two pretty girls in black silk gowns, a stripling
with curly hair, and a ridiculously small donkey.
At the end of a few miles, this last appeared so
tired that Shelley and Jane had to carry him.
In the village where they slept they sold him to
a peasant and bought a mule in his place.

The whole of the district had been devastated
by the war, the villages were half-destroyed, the
houses mostly roofless with fire-blackened beams;
if they asked a farmer for milk he replied by
cursing the Cossacks who had carried off his
cows.

In the wretched inns the beds were so dirty
that Mary and Jane dared not use them. Enormous rats brushed by them in the darkness. They
fell into the habit of sitting up all night in the
farm-kitchens. The big stove, still alight, made
the atmosphere heavy, and between sleeping and
waking, the crying of children and the creak-
ings of the old woodwork were woven into their
dreams. Mary thought of her father, and wondered whether or not he was suffering terribly
from her flight. Shelley was preoccupied with
the fate of Harriet.

From Troyes he wrote her a long letter, urging her to come out and join them in Switzerland. She should live near them, and there, at
least, find one firm and constant friend. He
162

gave her news of Mary's health, which appeared to him a natural thing to do, and he felt quite sure that Harriet would very soon be with them. Maybe, the "world" would think this life in common immoral, but why trouble about "the world's" opinion? Was it not better to obey the dictates of love and kindness than those of absurd prejudices? Harriet made no reply.

Going by Pontarlier and Neufchâtel they reached the Lake of the Four Cantons. Shelley wished to settle at Brunnen, near the Chapel of William Tell, the Defender of Liberty. The only empty house in the place was an old château, deserted, and falling into ruin. They hired two rooms in it for six months, and bought furniture, beds, chairs, wardrobes, and a stove. The curé and the village doctor came to call upon the newcomers, and on the same day Shelley began to write a great novel, *The Assassins*. They had settled down "for ever."

But the new stove refused to draw, and Shelley, who was not clever with his fingers, tinkered at it in vain. The room was glacial and filled with smoke. Outside the rain beat against the windows. The three young exiles found themselves desperately lonely. They recalled the comfort of English houses, English tea, hot and scented, England's mild sky, the cool, good-natured Englishmen speaking their language and able to pronounce their names. Even the English usurers, though of course rapacious, were always courteous.

Shelley counted up the common purse. There remained just twenty-eight pounds. The same eager desire rose in all three, which Shelley expressed by the words "Let's go home!"

No sooner said than the decision was taken, and their spirits rose. "Most laughable to think," writes Jane, "of our going to England the second day after entering a new house for six months, and all because the stove don't suit! As we left Dover, and England's white cliffs disappeared, I thought I should never see them again, and now . . ." Having made up their minds at midnight, the next morning, in driving rain, they took a boat to Lucerne. Great was the surprise of Brunnen's curé when he learnt that they were gone.

From Lucerne they reached Bâsle by passenger boat and thence on to Cologne. The weather was delightful. Beneath the evening stars, the boatmen chanted love-songs. Shelley worked at *The Assassins*. Mary and Jane had each started a novel, too, and the hills crowned with ruins on either side gave them a good background for the romantic adventures of their heroes.

Then the Dutch mail-coach carried them through a sleepy land of comfortable wooden houses, canals, and windmills. When they reached Rotterdam they were again penniless. After long discussion, a ship's Captain agreed to take them aboard. The sea was as rough as on the day of their departure.

Shelley employed his time arguing the question of slavery with one of the passengers. Mary and Jane backed him up with warmth. They did not know in the least if they would have anything to eat the next day, but they did know that Percy was a genius, and that Man is perfectible,

CHAPTER XX

THE PARIAHS

ON arriving in London, Shelley could not pay the cab fare, so with Mary, Jane, and the trunks, he drove round to his bankers, merely to learn that Harriet had withdrawn the entire balance to his credit. At this news the two girls were highly indignant. The only way to get out of the scrape, and avoid the police-station, was to go and see Harriet herself. Shelley had her address, and thither they now drove. Harriet thought at first that her husband had come back to her, and was very indignant, in her turn, when she knew that her rival was waiting below at the door. However, she lent Shelley a few pounds, which enabled the three wanderers to take furnished lodgings in a mean street.

Things looked black. Godwin absolutely refused to see them. Shelley pleaded that he had given a practical application to the principles of *Political Justice,* but this merely exasperated the author of the treatise still more. *Political Jus-*
166

tice was in his eyes a theoretical work, the principles of which might be excellent in some Utopia —although it was also very long since he had written it—but in London, in the midst of a pitiless society, in his own house, to expose Godwin and his only daughter to the scorn of his friends, thus to pervert his teaching . . . No, he would never forgive them.

When he mentioned the adventure it was in the most severe terms. Writing to a Mr. John Taylor of Norwich, he said:

"I have a story to tell you of the deepest melancholy. . . . You are already acquainted with the name of Shelley. . . . Not to keep you longer in suspense, he, a married man, has run away with my daughter. I cannot conceive of an event of more accumulated horror.

"Mary, my only daughter, was absent in Scotland for her health, and returned to me on the 30th of March last. Shelley came to London on the 18th June and I invited him to take his meals at my house. On Sunday, June 26th, he accompanied Mary and her sister, Jane Clairmont, to the tomb of Mary's mother, and there it seems the impious idea first occurred to him of seducing her. . . . He had the madness to disclose his plans to me and to ask my consent. I expostulated with him with all the energy of which I was master. . . . I seemed to have succeeded, but in the night of the 27th July, Mary and her sister Jane escaped from my house, and the next morning when I rose I found a letter on my dressing table informing me what they had done."

He begged Taylor to preserve the utmost secrecy about the affair, so that no stigma may be attached to the names of these unfortunate girls. "When I use the word stigma I am sure it is wholly unnecessary to say that I apply it in a very different sense to the two girls. Jane has been guilty of an indiscretion only . . . Mary has been guilty of a crime."

Yet Shelley, in former days, had borrowed large sums to lend to Mary's father, and on this account the bailiffs, so soon as they heard of his return, had begun to dun him. Godwin not only was unable to repay Shelley, but had fresh need of money himself, and it was these financial questions which compelled him, most reluctantly, to continue a correspondence with a depraved and perfidious young man. His conscience suffered greatly.

So much hypocrisy in a man they had so venerated, was grievous to Mary and Shelley. "Oh,

philosophy!" they said, and sighed. As to Mrs.
Godwin, she reproached them above all with cor-
rupting her daughter, and she forbade the gentle
Fanny to visit them. She herself went to see
Jane once, but meeting Shelley on the stairs she
turned away her head.

Their intercourse with Harriet was sometimes
easy, sometimes difficult, according to her
changes of mood. She wanted for nothing, having still some of Shelley's money, besides receiving an allowance from the old tavern-keeper,
but she was with child and very unhappy. She
passed her days in telling her story to the gossips of the neighbourhood, or in writing in pathetic phrases to her friend Catherine Nugent,
the Dublin dressmaker:

"Every age has its cares. God knows I have
mine. Dear Ianthe is quite well. She is fourteen months old and has six teeth. What I
should have done without this dear babe and my
sister I know not. This world is a scene of
heavy trials to us all. I little expected ever to
go thro' what I have. But time heals the deepest wounds, and for the sake of that sweet in-
fant I hope to live many years. Write to me
often. . . . Tell me how you are in health. Do
not despond, though I see nothing to hope for

when all that was virtuous becomes vicious and depraved. So it is—nothing is certain in this world. I suppose there is another, where those that have suffered keenly here will be happy. Tell me what you think of this. My sister is with me. I wish you knew her as well as I do. She is worthy of your love. Adieu, dear friend, may you still be happy is the first wish of your ever faithful friend,

"H. SHELLEY.

"Ianthe is well and very engaging."

Sometimes she was full of hope. Her friends told her that love-affairs of this sort were short-lived and that her husband would come back to her. Then she felt gay and wrote Shelley friendly letters. She was sure that it was Mary who had made all the mischief: that she had seduced Percy by telling him extravagant tales: that in reality he was good, that he would never desert her and his two children.

At other times she had fits of depression and rage. Then she did all she knew to make the life of the hated couple more difficult still. She ran into debt, and sent the creditors to Shelley. She declared that he was living in promiscuity with two of Godwin's daughters. She found out Godwin's creditors in order to urge them to be

170

pitiless, and Mary, who had never seen her, would say with a sigh: "That frightful woman!"

One day in November, Harriet was in a state of discomfort and pain, and imagined herself very ill. Her first thought at such moments was always to call her husband. She sent for Shelley during the night and he came at once. Without again becoming the lover, he would have liked to remain her most devoted friend. But, not understanding the shade of difference, the moment he showed attention, she would try to caress him. Then he would check her with gentle firmness.

At the end of November, she gave birth to a boy, an eight-months' child. It brought about no reconciliation. Shelley doubted if the child was his.

With Mary, in spite of their misfortunes, he was deliciously happy. They shared the same tastes, and both looked upon Life as an opportunity for learning prolonged into old age. They read the same books and often aloud. She went with him in his visits to his lawyers, or the sheriff's officers. When he amused himself by the Serpentine, just as he used to do at Oxford, in launching a paper flotilla, Mary, sitting beside him, fashioned the boats with tireless fingers.

Under his direction, she set herself to learn

Latin and even Greek. More cultured than
Harriet, she did not see in these studies, as did
the first Mrs. Shelley, a rather boring game, but
an extension of her enjoyment. The greatest
charm of literary culture is that it humanizes
love. Catullus, Theocritus, and Petrarch united
to render more exquisite our lover's kisses. Shelley, watching his new companion at work, was
filled with admiration for her strength of character, and was delighted to consider her as much
superior to himself.

The only shadow, and that a light one, was the
presence of Jane, or rather of Claire, for, having
decided that her name was ugly, she had changed
it for another which was more to her taste. A
brilliant and beautiful girl, she suffered from
nerves and was terribly susceptible. Nothing
was worse for her than to live in close contact
with an amorous young couple. She had a passionate admiration for Percy, and showed it a
little too plainly. Mary complained, but Shelley
could not agree that there was anything in the
sentiment either disagreeable or shocking.

He hated being alone, so when Mary, who was
expecting a child, had to give up walks and late
hours, he took Claire with him to the lawyers, the
bailiffs, and the banks of the Serpentine, and
every day he begged her to pass the evening with

him. He talked to her of Harriet, of Miss Hitchener, and of his sisters. He had always loved confidential talks, and long analyses of thought; sincerity appeared to him easy with Claire because she was not his mistress. But Mary could not conceal her impatience, and Claire, vexed by her sister's reproaches, remained silent and gloomy a whole day through.

In the evening when Mary had gone to bed, Shelley undertook to pacify Claire. Cleverly and patiently he explained until midnight the somewhat complicated sentiments of their little group. Such was his gentle kindness that Claire ceased to sulk.

"But I've suffered so much!" she said.

"Imaginary sufferings, my dear Claire! You misunderstand words and gestures to which Mary attaches no importance whatever."

"All the same, I have really suffered, but how I like good, kind, explaining people!"

Shelley went up to repeat the conversation to Mary. In the room overhead they heard Claire talking and walking in her sleep. Presently she came down, she was feeling terribly nervous, and could not remain alone. Mary took her into her own bed, and Shelley went to sleep upstairs.

This little scene with slight variations was often repeated. Claire's nervousness was communicated to Shelley. Having talked of ghosts and hobgoblins the greater part of the night, they ended by frightening each other.

"What is the matter with you, Claire? You're deathly pale. . . . Your eyes . . . No! Don't look at me like that!"

"You, too, Percy, you look strange . . . the air is heavy, full of monsters . . . don't let us stay here any longer!"

They said good night and went to their rooms, but almost immediately after, Shelley and Mary heard a loud cry; somebody tumbled down the stairs, and Claire, with disordered features, came to relate that her pillow had been pulled from under her head by an invisible hand.

Shelley listened to the tale with terrified interest, but Mary shrugged her shoulders. If only this crazy girl would take herself off!

. . . .

The outcasts saw few friends. The Boinville-Newton set, despite their broad-minded French philosophy, had turned a cold shoulder when they were told by Shelley of his new life. With them, as with Godwin, actions did not run on all fours with speech, and indulgence in theory allied itself for some mysterious reason with inclemency in practice. On the other hand it was the sceptical Hogg and Peacock who came at the first call. They believed in the innocence of Harriet, and did not approve of Shelley's conduct, but they were full of human interest, and looked upon the passion of love as a somewhat comic disease.

Shelley had invited Hogg with misgivings. He was afraid such a cynic would not please the two girls. Nor was Mary's first impression favourable. "He's amusing enough when he jokes," she said, "but the moment he treats of a serious subject, one sees that his point of view is altogether wrong."

Hogg, in fact, became every day more British and conservative, singing the praises of tradition, sport, Public Schools, and naming the best port-wine years. But finding Mary very pretty and intelligent, he told Shelley so, who repeated it to her. On Hogg's next visit she thought him much more sympathetic. No doubt he spoke of virtue as a blind man does of colours; in this family of enthusiastic "souls" he was the "hardened sinner"; but his charm was acknowledged. Mary thought his coldness a cloak, and that he was better than he appeared. He was afraid to be sincere with himself or to delve deep, which would have driven him to forgo so many things that he liked, but he was really too intelligent not to feel the weakness of his position.

175

Being both good-natured and cultivated, he was ready to give a helping hand to Mary and Claire in translating Ovid or Anacreon, when their usual master had mysteriously vanished. He also accompanied the ladies to their bonnet-maker without grumbling, for they, too, visited bonnet-shops just like poor Harriet, although they went in quite another frame of mind. If she bought bonnets with rapture, Mary bought them with a lofty condescension, so that Shelley did not even have to excuse in her a concession to fashion which she herself was the first to deplore.

CHAPTER XXI

GODWIN

THE lodging-house servant brought up a letter from a lady who was waiting on the opposite pavement. It was from Fanny, to warn Shelley that his creditors were plotting to have him arrested. He and Mary ran down to the street, but, on seeing them, Fanny hastened away. She was in terror of Godwin, who had forbidden all communication with the outcasts, and she, perhaps, had cared too much for Percy to wish to see him again now that he belonged to her sister. But, being a swift runner, he soon caught up with her. She told him the bailiffs were looking for him, that it was his publisher who had given them his address, and that Godwin wouldn't lift a finger to save him.

Not having money to free himself, the only thing he could do was to disappear. He decided to find another lodging while Mary and Claire should remain quietly where they were, so as to trick the enemy. Thus, for the first time, the

lovers had to separate, a separation which seemed
terrible to both. They were forced to make ap-
pointments in out-of-the-way taverns, to take a
few stealthy kisses, and to part immediately, lest
Mary might be followed. On Sundays, when
arrests are illegal, they remained together till
midnight.

One evening the courage to separate failed
them, and Mary followed Shelley into a miserable hotel. The landlord looked with a suspicious
eye on this couple who had no luggage, and refused to serve them with a meal unless they paid
him in advance. Shelley sent round to Peacock,
and while waiting for the money took out the
pocket-Shakespeare he always carried, and read
aloud to Mary *Troïlus and Cressida*. It made
them forget their hunger a whole day through.
Next morning at breakfast-time Peacock, penniless himself, sent them some cakes. If life was
difficult there was joy in suffering together.
Love and misfortune made a happy pair.

When they were apart, waiting for night-time,
they sent each other, by a confidential messenger,
tender little notes, scribbled in haste.

"Oh! my dearest love," wrote Shelley, "why
are our pleasures so short and so interrupted?
How long is this to last? . . . Meet me to-morrow at three o'clock in St. Paul's if you do not
178

hear before. Adieu: remember love at vespers before sleep. I do not omit *my* prayers."

"Good night, my love," replied Mary, "to-morrow I will seal this blessing on your lips. Dear good creature, press me to you, and hug your own Mary to your heart. Perhaps she will one day have a father: till then be everything to me, love, and indeed I will be a good girl and never vex you. I will learn Greek and—but when shall we meet when I may tell you all this, and you will so sweetly reward me?"

In January, 1815, this trying existence was brought to an end by an event they had long expected without desiring it, but which they also accepted without any hypocritical regret. Old Sir Bysshe died at the age of eighty-three. Timothy Shelley became second baronet, and Percy, the direct heir.

He set out for his father's house, accompanied by Claire, who was in a state of great excitement and eager curiosity. Sir Timothy, puffed up with his new title, and more indignant than ever that a baronet should have such a son, refused him admission to Field Place by the footman. He sat down on the doorstep and read *Comus* from Mary's pocket-copy of Milton.

Presently the doctor came out to tell him his father was greatly incensed with him. Then, his cousin, Shelley Sidney, stealthily appeared to give the Prodigal Grandson details of the Will.

A most extraordinary Will. The fixed idea of old Sir Bysshe had been to found an enormous hereditary fortune, and for that purpose to increase the entailed estates as much as possible. He left, in real and personal property, possessions which probably did not fall short of £200,000. One portion of this, valued at £80,000, formed the estate entail which must necessarily pass to Percy on his father's death. But Sir Bysshe desired that this accumulation of his long life should be kept together by his descendants, and should pass from eldest son to eldest son through future generations of Shelleys. For this purpose, the consent and signature of his grandson were necessary, and he had hoped to obtain them in the following manner. If Percy would concur in prolonging the entail, and further, would agree to entail the unsettled estate, he should, after his father's death, enjoy the usufruct of the entire fortune. If he should refuse, then he would only inherit, always after the death of Sir Timothy, the £80,000 of which it was impossible to deprive him.

Shelley went back to London musing over this strange news, and called on his solicitor to dis-

cuss it with him. He did not feel he could consent to the extension of the entail, since he disapproved of all such plutocratic legislation: nor
did he desire, either for himself or his children,
the ownership of so huge a fortune. What he
wanted was an immediate income sufficient to
live on, according to his inclinations, and a certain sum down, so as to settle his debts. To se-
cure these moneys, he proposed, through his
lawyer, to sell to his father the reversion of the
settled estates. The proposal pleased Sir Timothy, who had abandoned all hope of ever bringing Percy to heel, and who now thought only of
his second son, John. Unfortunately the lawyers
were not sure that the arrangement was legally
possible under the terms of the Will. These only
authorized the re-sale by Percy to his father of
the estate of a grand-uncle, valued at £18,000.
This transaction took place and Shelley received
in exchange an income of one thousand pounds
a year during the joint lives of Sir Timothy and
himself, and in addition three thousand pounds
were advanced by Sir Timothy towards the payment of his son's debts. If this was not a big
fortune, it was at least the end of straitened
means, of furnished lodgings, and of duns.

His first thought was to make Harriet an allowance. He promised her £200 a year, which,

in addition to the £200 which her father allowed her, should be sufficient for all her wants. Next he undertook to pay off Godwin's debts, and set apart for that purpose the whole of his first year's annuity.

The "venerated friend" found the offer of one thousand pounds far below his expectations. To hear him talk, nothing was easier than to borrow, on an inheritance now soon to fall in, the many thousands of pounds of which the Skinner Street book-shop stood so much in need.

Shelley, exasperated but courteous, informed Godwin, with an indignation which he restrained, of his surprise that Mary's father should think it proper to write to the seducer of his daughter to ask him for money, and at the same time to refuse to enter into any relations with that daughter herself, who was foolish enough to suffer from it. Godwin replied that it was precisely because he was borrowing money from the seducer that he could not receive Mary: his dignity would not allow it! He could not risk having it said that he had bartered his daughter's honour for the payment of his debts. His scruples were so exaggerated that he returned a cheque drawn by Shelley in his favour, with the remark that the names of Shelley and of Godwin must not figure on the same cheque. Shelley

182

could make it payable to Joseph Hume or James Martin, and then he, Godwin, might consent to cash it. On which the following letters were exchanged:

Shelley to Godwin

"I confess that I do not understand how the pecuniary engagements subsisting between us in any degree impose restrictions on your conduct towards me. They did not, at least to your knowledge or with your consent, exist at the period of my return from France, and yet your conduct towards me and your daughter was then precisely such as it is at present. . . .

"In my judgment, neither I, nor your daughter, nor her offspring, ought to receive the treatment which we encounter on every side. It has perpetually appeared to me to have been your especial duty to see that, so far as mankind value your good opinion, we were dealt justly by, and that a young family, innocent and benevolent and united, should not be confounded with prostitutes and seducers. My astonishment, and I will confess when I have been treated with most harshness and cruelty by you, my indignation has been extreme, that, knowing, as you do, my nature, any considerations should have prevailed on you to have been thus harsh and cruel. Do

not talk of forgiveness again to me, for my blood
boils in my veins, and my gall rises against all
that bears the human form, when I think of what
I, their benefactor and ardent lover, have endured of enmity and contempt from you and
from all mankind."

Godwin to Shelley

"I am sorry to say that your letter—this moment received—is written in a style the very
opposite of conciliation, so that if I were to answer it in the same style we should be involved
in a controversy of inextinguishable bitterness.
As long as understanding and sentiment shall
exist in this frame, I shall never cease from my
disapprobation of that act of yours which I regard as the great calamity of my life."

Shelley to Godwin

"We will confine our communications to
business. . . .

"I plainly see how necessary immediate advances are to your concerns, and will take care
that I shall fail in nothing which I can do to
procure them."

The cold contempt of this letter did not dis-
courage the borrower.

CHAPTER XXII

DON JUAN CONQUERED

MARY'S child was born before its time, and the doctor said it would not live. Shelley kept watch between the cradle and the bed in company with Livy and Seneca. Fanny came round with baby-clothes sent by Mrs. Godwin in her capricious way, but the Philosopher remained inflexible. Hogg dropped in to gossip, to tell the great news of the day, the return from Elba, and he did Mary good by his common sense and sarcasm. With a temperature, and always in the society of Shelley, she had the rather terrifying if pleasant impression of slipping away out of life. Hogg brought her back to a sense of reality.

In spite of predictions, the child did live and grew. Mary had begun to feel easy about it when, at the end of the month, she found on waking one morning that it was dead. This was a great sorrow.

Shelley and Claire continued their walks together, while Mary stayed at home. She sat knitting and thinking of her little child. "I was a mother, and am so no longer," she kept repeating, and at night she dreamed that the baby was not dead, and that by rubbing it before the fire they had brought it back to life. Then she awoke to find the cradle empty. From the streets floated up the hoarse shouting of crowds. It was a time of riots. France threatened war. Mary saw everything through a mist of tears.

Claire's presence in the house vexed her more and more. She was certain that Claire was in love with Shelley, had always been in love with him. Percy's loyalty was self-evident, his morality super-human, angelic; but he thought it possible to read Petrarch with an impassioned girl, to direct her studies, to sit up with her the whole night through, without danger. Mary said to herself: "My charming Shelley understands the elves better than he does women."

When she was alone with him in the evening, she confessed her jealousy. It was a sentiment he could not understand. He thought it base, and that it belittled his divine Mary. He knew his capacity for love to be infinite, and that in dividing it with another woman he took away nothing from his mistress. The company of the wild and brilliant Claire was very precious to him, but he had to acknowledge that the atmos-

186

phere of this three-fold union was becoming irrespirable.

Mary besought him to send Claire away. "Your friend," as she now always called her. They tried, during many weeks, to find a place for her as governess or companion, but the unfortunate reputation which her flight to France had earned her rendered all such attempts futile.

Claire herself had not the smallest desire to leave. She delighted in her intellectual intimacy with Percy, and she awaited its inevitable result without fear. Finally, however, Mary's gentle firmness carried the day, and it was arranged that Claire should go to Lynmouth, and lodge there with a friend of Godwin's, a Mrs. Bricknell, a widow.

Mary's Journal

"*Friday.*—Not very well. After breakfast read Spenser. Shelley goes out with his friend, he returns first. Construe Ovid—90 lines—Jefferson Hogg returns. Read over the Ovid to Jefferson. Shelley and the lady walk out. After tea talk. Shelley and his friend have a last conversation.

"*Saturday.*—Claire goes; Shelley walks with her. Jefferson does not come till five. Gets very anxious about Shelley, goes out to meet him.

187

returns: it rains. Shelley returns at half-past six; the business is finished. Read Ovid. Charles Clairmont comes to tea. Talk of pictures. I begin a new journal with our regeneration."

. . . .

Claire, exiled to the country, enjoyed after such storm and stress her first days of profound peace. But she was not the girl to put up for long with rural solitude. She must have a reason for living—and she did not fail to find one.

When people are in love they always imagine, quite wrongly, that it is because they have come across an exceptional being who has inspired them with the passion. The truth is that love, existing already in the soul, seeks out a suitable object and, if it does not find one, then creates it. But if, in an ordinary girl, this love-seeking is unconscious, it was otherwise with the brilliant and hot-blooded Claire. Realizing the impossibility of taking Shelley from her sister, or even of sharing him with her, she deliberately looked round for some other hero on whom to expend her unemployed affection. Some women in such cases send letters to great writers, or soldiers, or actors. But Claire, who was poetical, desired a poet.

She found none more worthy of her than George Gordon, Lord Byron, the man the most

worshipped and the most hated in the whole of
England. She knew his poems by heart, Shelley
had so often read them to her with enthusiasm.
She knew the stories of vice and wit, of diabolical charm and infernal cruelty which were woven
round his name.

His extraordinary beauty, his title, his genius
as a writer, the boldness of his ideas, the scandals
of his love affairs, all contributed to make of him
the perfect hero. He had had mistresses among
the highest in the land, the Countess of Oxford,
Lady Frances Webster, and the unfortunate
Lady Caroline Lamb, who the first day that she
met him wrote in her journal: "Mad, bad and
dangerous to know": and then underneath, "But
this pale handsome face holds my destiny."

He had married, and all London repeated the
tale that, when he got into the carriage after the
ceremony, he said to Lady Byron: "You are
now my wife, and that is enough for me to hate
you. Were you some one else's wife, I might
perhaps care about you." He had treated her
with such contempt that she had been driven to
ask for a separation from him at the end of the
first year.

Claire, who sought only for difficult adventures, and had supreme confidence in herself,

found out Byron's address and decided to chance her luck.

Claire to Byron

"An utter stranger takes the liberty of addressing you. . . . It is not charity I demand, for of that I stand in no need. . . . I tremble with fear at the fate of this letter. I cannot blame if it shall be received by you as an impudent imposture. It may seem a strange assertion, but it is not the less true that I place my happiness in your hands. . . . If a woman, whose reputation has yet remained unstained, if without either guardian or husband to control, she should throw herself on your mercy, if with a beating heart she should confess the love she has borne you many years, if she should return your kindness with fond affection and unbounded devotion, could you betray her, or would you be silent as the grave? . . . I must entreat your answer without delay. Address me as E. Trefusis, 21 Noley Place, Mary le Bonne."

Don Juan made no reply. This unknown writer of ornate style was small game for him. But there is no one more tenacious than a woman tired of her virtue. Claire returned to the attack a second time. "Sunday Morning. Lord Byron is requested to state whether seven o'clock this evening will be convenient to him to receive a lady to communicate with him on business of peculiar importance. She desires to be admitted alone and with the utmost privacy."

Lord Byron sent out word by the servant that he had left town.

Then Claire wrote in her own name that, wanting to go on the stage, and knowing that Lord Byron was interested in Drury Lane Theatre, she would like to ask his advice. Byron's reply was to recommend her to call on the stage manager. Undeterred, she made, at once, a skilful change of front. It was not a theatrical career but the literary life which she now desired. She had written half a novel and would so very much like to submit it to Byron's judgment. As he continued to keep silence, or to send evasive replies, she risked offering him the only thing which a man with any self-respect seldom refuses.

"I may appear to you imprudent, vicious, but one thing at least time shall show you, that I love gently and with affection, that I am incapable of anything approaching to the feeling of revenge or malice. I do assure you your future shall be mine.

"Have you any objection to the following plan? On Thursday evening we may go out of town together by some stage or mail about the distance of ten or twelve miles. There we shall be free and unknown; we can return early the following morning. I have arranged everything here so that the slightest suspicion may not be excited. Pray do so with your people.

"Will you admit me for two moments to *settle* with you *where?* Indeed, I will not stay an instant after you tell me to go. . . . Do what you will or go where you will, refuse to see me and behave unkindly, I shall ever remember the gentleness of your manners and the wild originality of your countenance."

It was then that Don Juan, trapped and tired by the long pursuit, decided to accept his defeat. He had already decided to leave England and fix himself in Switzerland or Italy, and the prospect of a speedy departure set welcome limits to this unwelcome affair.

CHAPTER XXIII

ARIEL AND DON JUAN

DON JUAN counted, however, without the energy of Elvira. Claire had made up her mind to follow him to Switzerland, and this dark-eyed girl was a flame and a force. She arranged that the Shelleys should chaperon her, knowing that they, too, would welcome the idea of a change.

Since she left them, they had been living at Bishopsgate, on the border of Windsor Forest, and beneath the oak-shades of the Great Park Shelley had composed his first long poem since *Queen Mab.* This was *Alastor, or the Spirit of Solitude,* an imaginative interpretation of his spiritual experiences, and a record of the exquisite mountain, river, and woodland scenery of the past year. The tone differs from that of his previous works. Melancholy and resignation soften down the confident assertions of earlier years, and religious and moral theories, if still serving as a peg, get somewhat pushed into the background.

In the preface he shows the Poet thirsting for love and dying because he cannot find it. But, says Shelley, it is better to die than to live as do the comfortable worldlings, "who, deluded by no generous error, instigated by no sacred thirst of doubtful knowledge, duped by no illustrious superstition, loving nothing on this earth, and cherishing no hopes beyond—yet keep aloof from sympathies with their kind, rejoicing neither in human joy, nor mourning with human grief; these and such as they have their appointed curse. . . . They are morally dead. They are neither friends, nor lovers, nor fathers, nor citizens of the world, nor benefactors of their country . . . they live unfruitful lives, and prepare for their old age a miserable grave."

While Shelley had no regrets for his actions, all the same, life in England had become odious to him. Mary, as an unmarried wife, suffered from her social ostracism, and thought that if they went abroad, where their story would be unknown, she would have more chance of making friends.

She had given birth to a second child in January, 1816, a fine little boy whom she had named William, after Godwin. The expenses of the household, with the addition of a nurse, were heavy, the income small. Life in Switzerland was said to be cheap; Claire, at least, had little difficulty in persuading her that it was so.

As in the time of their first flight from London, the extraordinary trio crossed France, Burgundy, the Jura, and, reaching Geneva, settled down at Sécheron, one of its suburbs, in the Hôtel d'Angleterre. The house was on the edge of the lake, from its windows they saw the sun sparkling on every wave-crest of the blue water, and in the distance the black mountain ridges that seemed to quiver in the sunny atmosphere. Farther away still, a brilliant and solid-looking white cloud spoke of the snow peaks of the Alps. The change to this golden climate after English greyness and London gloom was delicious. They hired a boat, and passed long days upon the water, reading and sleeping.

.   .   .   .

While they lived thus, a band of happy children, with the blue sky above them, and the blue lake beneath, *Childe Harold* in the most sumptuous of travelling carriages was crossing Flanders on his way to join them. England, in one of those crazy fits of virtue which alternate with periods of the most amazing licence, had just hounded Byron from her shores. When he entered a ball-room every woman would leave it, as though he were the devil in person. He determined to shake for ever from his shoes the dust of so hypocritical a land.

His departure was accompanied by the most frenzied curiosity. Society, which punishes cruelly any revolt of the elemental instincts, nevertheless, in her heart of hearts, admires the rebel and envies him. At Dover where the Pilgrim embarked, a double line of spectators stood on either side of the gangway. Great ladies borrowed the clothes of their chambermaids, so as to mix unobserved with the crowd. People pointed out to one another the enormous packing-cases containing his sofa, his books, his services of china and glass.

The sea was rough, and Byron reminded his travelling companions that his grandfather Admiral Byron was nicknamed "Foul-weather Jack" because he never put to sea without a squall blowing up. He took a certain pleasure in painting his own portrait against this traditional stormy background. Unfortunate, he would have his misfortunes transcendent.

. . . .

A few days later there was great commotion at the Hôtel d'Angleterre. Every one was on edge expecting the arrival of the noble lord. Claire was tremulous in spite of her audacity, Shelley in the happiest spirits was impatient. He was not shocked by the affair between Byron and Claire. On the contrary he hoped to see the same ties formed between Byron and his sister-in-law as existed between himself and Mary.

The Shelleys were not disappointed by Byron's first appearance. His beauty was extraordinary. To begin with you were struck by his air of pride and intellect; next you noticed the moonlight paleness of his skin, his splendid dark blue eyes, his black and slightly curling hair, the perfect line of his eyebrows. The nose and chin were firm and well-drawn, the mouth full and voluptuous. His only defect appeared in his walk. "Club-footed" was said of him. "Cloven-footed" he insinuated of himself, for he preferred to be considered diabolic rather than infirm. Mary saw that his lameness embarrassed him, for whenever he had to take a few steps before spectators he made some satanic jest. In the register-book of the hotel, against the word "age" he wrote "a hundred."

Byron and Shelley got on well together. Byron was glad to find Shelley a man of his own class, who in spite of hardships had retained the charming ease of manner peculiar to the young man of good birth. The culture of this spirit astounded Byron. He, too, had read enormously, but without Shelley's serious application. Shelley had read to know, Byron had read to dazzle, and Byron was perfectly well aware of the difference. He felt, too, the instant conviction that Shelley's will was a force, a bent bow, while his own floated loose on the current at the mercy of his passions and of his mistresses.

Shelley, the least vain of men, did not observe this admiration for him, which Byron took care to hide. While listening to the third canto of *Childe Harold* he was moved to enthusiasm and discouragement. In the superb energy of the poem, which rose and swelled, irresistibly like a flood, he recognized genius and despaired of ever equalling it.

But if the poet filled him with admiration, the man filled him with astonishment. He had expected a Titan in revolt, and he found a wounded aristocrat fully alive to the pleasures and pains of vanity, which seemed to Shelley so puerile. Byron had outraged convention, but, all the same he believed in it. It had stood in the path of his desires, and he had flung it aside, but with regret. That which Shelley had done ingenuously, he had done consciously. Banished from society, he valued nothing so much as social success. A bad husband, it was only to legitimate love that he paid respect. His mouth overflowed with cynicism, but it was by way of reprisals, not from conviction. Between marriage and depravity he recognized no middle path. He had sought to terrify his compatriots by acting an audacious part, but only because he had despaired of conquering them by acting a traditional one.

Shelley looked to women as a source of exaltation, Byron as a pretext for idling. Shelley angelic, too angelic, venerated them. Byron human, too human, desired them and talked of them in the most contemptuous fashion. "It is the plague of these women," said he, "that you can not live with them or without them. . . . I cannot make up my mind whether or not women have souls. My beau-ideal would be a woman with talent enough to understand and value mine, but not sufficient to be able to shine herself."

The upshot of certain of their conversations was surprising. Shelley, mystical without knowing it, managed to scandalize Byron, a Don Juan in spite of himself.

This did not prevent them from being excellent company one for the other. When Shelley, always a great fisher of souls, tried to win over his friend to a less futile conception of life, Byron defended his point of view by brilliant paradoxes

199

which delighted Shelley the artist, as much as
they pained Shelley the moralist. Both were
passionately fond of the water. They bought a
boat, keeled and clinker-built, in which they went
on the lake every evening with Mary, Claire, and
Byron's medical attendant, the handsome young
Italian, Polidori. Byron and Shelley, sitting silent, would ship their oars to follow with their
gaze fleeting shapes amidst the moon-lit clouds:
Claire would sing, and her warm, delicious voice
carried their thoughts with it over the starry
waters in a voluptuous flight.

One night of strong wind Byron, defying the
storm, said he would sing them an Albanian song.
"Now be sentimental and give me all your attention." It was a strange wild howl that he gave
forth, laughing the while at their disappointment, who had expected a wild Eastern melody.
From that day onward Mary and Claire named
him "the Albaneser," and "Albé" for short.

The two poets made a literary pilgrimage
round the lake. They visited the spot where
Rousseau has placed his *Nouvelle Héloïse,*
"Clarens, sweet Clarens, birthplace of deep
Love"; and Lausanne and Ferney, full of mem-
ories of Gibbon and Voltaire.

Shelley's enthusiasm gained Byron, who wrote
under its influence some of his finest lines. Near
209

Meillerie one of the sudden lake-storms nearly upset the boat. Byron began to strip. Shelley, who could not swim, sat still with folded arms. His calmness increased Byron's admiration for him, although he hid it more carefully than ever. Long afterwards Shelley, speaking of this storm, said, "I knew that my companion would try to save me, and it was a humiliating idea."

Sick of hotel life and the impertinent curiosity of their fellow-boarders, the Shelleys hired a cottage at Coligny on the edge of the lake. Byron settled himself at the Villa Diodati a short distance away. The two houses were only separated by a vineyard. Here, some vine-dressers at work in the early morning saw Claire come out of Byron's villa and run across to Shelley's. She lost a slipper on the way, but ashamed of being seen did not stop to pick it up. The honest Swiss peasants, chuckling hugely, made haste to carry the slipper of the English "Miss" to the mayor of the village.

Her love affair did not prosper. She was with child, and Byron was utterly tired of her. He let her see it. For a moment perhaps he had admired her voice, and her vivacity, but very soon she bored him. Nor did he feel himself in any way bound to this young woman who had thrust herself upon him with such pertinacity. . . .

" 'Carry off' quotha! and 'girl.' I should like to know *who* has been carried off except poor dear *me*. I have been more ravished myself than anybody since the Trojan War. I am accused of being hard on women. It may be so, but I have been their martyr. My whole life has been sacrificed *to* them and *by* them."

Shelley went to talk with him of Claire's future, and of the child's. As to Claire's, Byron was perfectly indifferent. All he wanted was to get rid of her as soon as possible and never to see her again. Shelley had nothing to say on this point, but he defended the rights of the unborn child.

At first Byron had the idea of confiding it to his sister Augusta. Claire refusing her consent, he then undertook to look after the child himself as soon as it was a year old, on condition that he should be absolutely master of it.

It became difficult for the Shelleys to remain in his neighbourhood. Not that there was any coldness between the two men, for while Shelley had found the negotiations for Claire painful, they had seemed to him perfectly natural. But Claire herself suffered, and Mary was often indignant at Byron's cynical talk. When he declared that women had no right to eat at the same table with men, that their proper place was in the harem or gynæceum, the daughter of Mary Wollstonecraft trembled with anger. Once more she was home-sick for English scenes. A house beside some English river now appeared to her, at this distance away, a haven of peace. Shelley wrote to his friends, Peacock and Hogg, to find something for them, and the journey home began.

. . . .

After they had gone, Byron wrote to his sister:

"Now don't scold; but what could I do? A foolish girl, in spite of all I could say or do, would come after me, or rather went before—for I found her here—and I had all the plague possible to persuade her to go back again, but at last she went. Now, dearest, I do most truly tell thee that I could not help this, that I did all I could to prevent it. I was not in love nor have any love left for any; but I could not exactly play the Stoic with a woman, who had scrambled eight hundred miles to unphilosophize me. . . . And now you know all that I know of the matter, and it's over."

Shelley remained in correspondence with Byron and did not give up hopes of "saving" him. Mingled with an immense deference for the great poet, Shelley's letters show a trace of haughty disapproval of the character of the man. He opposed to Byron's constant anxiety concerning his reputation, his success, and what was said of him in London, a picture of true glory.

"Is it nothing to create greatness and goodness, destined perhaps to infinite extensions? Is it nothing to become a source whence the minds of other men will draw strength and beauty? . . . What would Humanity be if Homer and Shakespeare had never written? . . . Not that I advise you to aspire to Fame. Your work should spring from a purer, simpler source. You should desire nothing more than to express your own thoughts, and to address yourself to the sympathy of those who are capable of thinking as you do. Fame follows those whom she is unworthy to guide."

Lord Byron, who was then on his way to Venice, read these lofty counsels with a weary indifference. Exacting veneration bored him.

CHAPTER XXIV

GRAVES IN THE GARDEN OF LOVE

OF the three young girls who had given life and gaiety to the house in Skinner Street one only, Fanny Imlay, was left. She alone, who was neither Godwin's child, nor yet Mrs. Godwin's, lived at home with them and called them "papa" and "mamma." She alone, so gentle and so loving, had found neither lover nor husband. Modest and unselfish, these are virtues which men praise—and pass by. For a moment she had wondered whether Percy would not think of her, and with a beating heart, had begun a correspondence with him. But Mary's hazel eyes had quenched the hopes to which the timid Fanny had never given definite form.

In this silent home, saddened by money worries, it was on Fanny that Mrs. Godwin wreaked her ill-humour, while Godwin let her understand that he could not continue to keep her, and that she ought to see about earning her own living. She asked nothing better, and would have liked to become a teacher, but the flight of Mary and Jane had thrown a mantle of disrepute over the household, and the heads of schools distrusted the way in which the Godwin girls had been brought up.

Sick at heart and with a touch of envy, Fanny admired from afar her sisters' life of wild adventure, a life which was sometimes dangerous, but always amusing. How she, too, would have loved to be over there at Lake Leman, in the company of the famous Lord Byron, of whom all London was talking!

"Is his face as fine as in your portrait of him? . . . Tell me also if he has a pleasing voice, for that has a great charm with me. Does he come into your house in a careless, friendly, dropping-in manner? I wish to know, though not from idle curiosity, whether he was capable of acting in the manner that London scandalmongers say he did. I cannot think from his writings that he can be such a *detestable being*. Do answer me these questions, for where I love the poet, I should like to respect the man.

"Shelley's boat excursion with him must have been very delightful. . . . I long very much to read the poem the 'Poet' has written on the spot where Julie was drowned. When will they be published in England? May I see them in manuscript? Say you have a friend who has few pleasures, and is very impatient to read them. . . . It is impossible to tell the good that POETS do their fellow creatures, at least those that can feel. Whilst I read I am a poet. I am inspired with good feelings—feelings that create perhaps a more permanent good in me than all the everyday preachments in the world; it counteracts the dross which one gives on the everyday concerns of life and tells us there is something yet in the world to aspire to—something by which succeeding ages may be made happy and perhaps better."

Mary and Claire would read these charming letters with a condescending pity. Poor Fanny! How she endured Skinner Street! Always thinking that Godwin's novels, Godwin's debts, and Mrs. Godwin's bad tempers were the most important things in the world! Fanny's slavery gave the two others a more vivid appreciation of their own freedom. Her loneliness enhanced for them the value of their lovers' society, and, in their compassion for her, Mary got Shelley to buy her a watch before leaving Geneva.

When the Shelleys and Claire came back to

England, to settle down at Bath, they saw Fanny as they passed through London. She was depressed, and spoke of nothing but her loneliness and her uselessness; no one wanted her. In saying good-bye to Shelley, her voice quivered. Yet she wrote to him at Bath with the same affectionate frankness as before, although her letters now had that indefinable note of reproach which those who lead a death-in-life feel towards those whose life is filled with living. Godwin, his literary work broken into by fresh money troubles, became more and more grumpy; an aunt, Everina Wollstonecraft, who had promised to take Fanny as governess in her school, wrote to say that a sister of Mary and Claire would certainly be too terrifying a teacher for the narrow-minded middle-class parents.

One morning the Shelleys received from Bristol a curious letter in which Fanny bade them farewell in mysterious sentences: "I am going to a place whence I hope never to return."

Mary implored Shelley to go to Bristol at once. He came home during the night without any news. Next morning he went again, and this time brought Mary lamentable tidings. Fanny had left Bristol for Swansea by the Cambrian Coach, and had put up at the Mackworth Arms Inn. She had gone at once to her room telling the chamber-maid that she was tired. When she did not come down next morning her door was forced, and she was found lying dead, her long brown hair spread about her. By her was the little Genevan watch given her by Mary and Shelley. On the table was a bottle of laudanum and the beginning of a letter:

"I have long determined that the best thing I could do was to put an end to the existence of a being whose birth was unfortunate, and whose life has only been a series of pain to those persons who have hurt their health in endeavouring to promote her welfare. Perhaps to hear of my death will give you pain, but you will soon have the blessing of forgetting that such a creature ever existed as . . ."

Godwin had taught in *Political Justice* that suicide is not a crime; the only difficulty being to decide in each individual case whether the social advantage of thirty supplementary years of life forbids recourse to a voluntary death. After the tragedy he wrote to Mary for the first time since her flight. It was to implore the three outcasts to avoid anything leading to publicity, "which to a mind in anguish is one of the severest of all trials."

Shelley's nerves were badly shaken by Fanny's terrible death, and Mrs. Godwin in her amiable way insinuated she had killed herself for love of him. He then remembered certain signs of emotion he had seen in her, and reproached himself for having always considered her as of a slightly lower status. Perhaps he had, though quite unwittingly, awakened her love at the moment when, deserted by Harriet, he sought a shelter in any feminine tenderness. Perhaps she had weighed and counted and analyzed with care, words and glances, into which he had meant to put mere friendliness. "How difficult it is to understand the soul of another! How much suffering one may cause without wishing it, or knowing it! How one may live in presence of the most profound, sometimes of the most despairful feelings without even suspecting their existence!" It does not suffice therefore to be sincere, nor to have good intentions. You can do just as much harm through not understanding as through unkindness. He was plunged into a blank despondency.

To shake it off, he went to spend a few days alone with a young literary critic, Leigh Hunt, who had praised his poetry with intelligence and enthusiasm. Hunt lived on Hampstead Heath in the Vale of Health, a spot as tree-embowered and almost as charming to-day as it was then. His wife Marianne was homely and hospitable. He had a whole brood of jolly children with whom Shelley could walk and play. There, he could forget for a time poor Fanny and Godwin. The visit was short but delicious, and he came home much cheered.

On his return, he found awaiting him a letter from Hookham, which he opened eagerly, for he had asked Hookham to find out for him what Harriet was doing. He had had no news of her for two months. She had drawn her allowance in March and in September, being then in her father's house. But since October nothing was known of her.

"My dear Sir," Hookham wrote, "It is nearly a month since I had the pleasure of receiving a letter from you, and you have no doubt felt surprised that I did not reply to it sooner. It was my intention to do so; but on enquiring, I found the utmost difficulty in obtaining the information you desire relative to Mrs. Shelley and your children.

"While I was yet endeavouring to discover Mrs. Shelley's address, information was brought me that she was dead—that she had destroyed herself. You will believe that I did not credit

211

the report. I called at the house of a friend of Mr. Westbrook; my doubt led to conviction. I was informed that she was taken from the Serpentine river on Tuesday last. . . . Little or no information was laid before the jury which sat on the body. . . . The verdict was *found drowned*. Your children are well and are both, I believe, in London."

Shelley went up to town in an agonizing condition of mind. With horror he saw in imagination the blond and child-like head, which he had so loved, befouled by the mud of the river-bed, green and swollen through its sojourn in the water. He asked himself how was it possible she could have abandoned her children and chosen so dreadful a death.

The Hunts and Hookham showed him every kindness, and told him all they knew. A paragraph in the *Times* stated: "On Thursday a respectable female far advanced in pregnancy was taken out of the Serpentine river, and brought home to her residence in Queen Street, Brompton, having been missed for nearly six weeks. She had a valuable ring on her finger. A want of honour in her own conduct is supposed to have led to this fatal catastrophe, her husband being abroad."

212

GRAVES IN THE GARDEN

The gossips of Queen Street repeated the little they had gleaned: Harriet no longer received letters from her husband, because her former landlady had failed to forward them, and she had given up all hope of his ever coming back to her. She had fallen, from despair. Living first with an army officer, he had been obliged to leave her on his regiment being ordered to India. Then, unable to endure the loneliness of life, she found a protector of humble grade, said to be a groom, and that he deserted her. The Westbrooks had deprived her of her children, and refused to receive her back. She was said to be in the family way, absolutely alone, and terrified at the approaching scandal. Then, came the body in the river.

Shelley passed an appalling night. . . . "Far advanced in pregnancy. . . ." What an end to her life . . . what madness. . . . Detailed and intimate memories of poor Harriet crowded back into his mind against his will, and he saw in imagination with terrible vividness the last scenes. . . . Harriet in love, Harriet in terror, Harriet in despair . . . every expression he knew too well. Ah, this name which during a few years had meant the whole world to him, for the future he must associate with all that is basest and most vile! "Harriet, my wife, a prostitute! Harriet, my wife, a suicide!"

There were moments when he asked himself if he were not responsible, but he pushed this idea from him with all his strength. "I did my duty. Always on every occasion in life, I have done what seemed to me the loyal and disinterested thing to do. When I left her, I no longer loved her. I assured her existence to the utmost of my means, and even beyond them. Never have I treated her with unkindness . . . it is those odious Westbrooks alone. . . . Ought I to have sacrificed my sanity and my life, to one who was unfaithful to me, and second-rate?"

His reason told him "No." Hogg and Peacock, who surrounded him with affectionate attentions, told him "No." He besought them to repeat it to him, for at instants he seemed to glimpse some mysterious and superhuman duty towards Harriet, in which he had failed. "In breaking traditional ties one sets free in man unknown forces, the consequences of which one cannot foresee. . . . Freedom is only good for the strong . . . for those who are worthy of it. . . . Harriet's soul was weak. . . ." Ah, little head, blond and childlike, of drowned Harriet. . . .

214

GRAVES IN THE GARDEN

Next day he wrote a tender letter to Mary, eager to dwell by contrast on her gentle serenity. He asked her to become a mother to his "poor babes, Ianthe and Charles." His counsel had just informed him that the Westbrooks would take action to contest his guardianship of the children, on the pretext that his irreligious opinions, and his living in concubinage with Miss Godwin, rendered him unfit to bring them up.

CHAPTER XXV

THE RULES OF THE GAME

IN what way does a marriage ceremony, religious or civil, add to the happiness of a pair of lovers, deeply smitten and full of confidence in one another? The event proved that it can at least make joy blossom on the countenance of a pedant. Godwin's exhibited an incredible satisfaction on learning that "the seducer" was going to make "an honest woman" of his daughter, and that, eventually, she would become Lady Shelley. He thus inspired in his ex-disciple a contempt for his character, full measure, pressed down, and running over.

At first there had been some hesitation as to whether it were decent to celebrate the marriage so soon after Harriet's death, but the authorities on social etiquette declared that it would not do to wait any longer for the Church's blessing on a union which Nature had already blessed twice over.

Just a fortnight after the body of the first

Mrs. Shelley had been taken out of the Serpentine, Mary and Percy were married by a clergyman in the church of St. Mildred, Bread Street. Godwin, beaming all over his face, and Mrs. Godwin, simpering and pretentious, signed as witnesses. That evening, for the first time since they ran away, the Shelleys dined in Skinner Street.

The family feast was a lugubrious one. There, in the little dining-room, Fanny had moved to and fro; there, Harriet had sat in her happy early wedded days; their ghosts, suffering and unsatisfied, continued to haunt the room and torture the living. It is true that Godwin's ill-temper had been changed by the morning's ceremony into an excess of urbanity, but too many memories troubled the guests to make any real cordiality possible.

That night Mary wrote in her journal: "Go to London. A marriage takes place. Draw. Read Lord Chesterfield and Locke." Mary had good nerves. Poor drowned Harriet was never a patch on her.

. . . .

Nevertheless, it was but right that the news of so splendid a marriage should be sent to every Godwin in the land. The Philosopher wrote to Hull Godwin:

"Dear Brother,

"Were it not that you have a family of your
own, and can see by them how little shrubs grow
into tall trees, you would hardly imagine that my
boy, born the other day, is now fourteen, and that
my daughter is between nineteen and twenty.
The piece of news I have to tell, however, is
that I went to church with this tall girl some
little time ago to be married. Her husband is
the eldest son of Sir Timothy Shelley, of Field
Place, in the county of Sussex, Baronet. So
that according to the vulgar ideas of the world
she is well married, and I have great hopes that
the young man will make her a good husband.
You will wonder, I daresay, how a girl without
a penny of fortune should make so good a match.
But such are the ups and downs of the world.
For my part, I care but little comparatively about
wealth, so that it should be her destiny in life
to be respectable, virtuous, and contented."

The letter closes with a word of cool thanks
for a ham and a turkey sent to the Skinner Street
household at Christmas.

But the formal marriage brought about one
real advantage. The "concubinage" argument,
advanced by those who wished to deprive Shelley
of his children, fell on the ground. The West-

brooks, however, did not give in. By the voice of the retired publican, the young Ianthe aged three, and Charles aged two, addressed a petition to the Lord Chancellor in which they said: "Our father avows himself to be an Atheist, and has written and published a certain work called *Queen Mab* with notes, and other works, wherein he blasphemously denies the existence of God as the Creator of the Universe, the sanctity of marriage, and all the most sacred principles of morality." For which reasons these precocious and virtuous infants prayed that their persons and fortunes might not be placed in the power of an unworthy father, but under the protection of persons of the highest morality, such as their maternal grandfather, and their kind Aunt Eliza.

Shelley's counsel took care to say nothing in defence of *Queen Mab:* there was nothing to be said at that time, and in that place, the Court of Chancery. He confined himself to denying the importance of a work written by a boy of nineteen.

"Notwithstanding Mr. Shelley's violent philippics against marriage, Mr. Shelley marries twice before he is twenty-five! He is no sooner liberated from the despotic chains which he speaks of with so much horror and contempt,

than he forges a new set, and becomes again a
willing victim of this horrid despotism! It is
hoped that a consideration of this marked difference between his opinions and his actions will
induce the Lord Chancellor not to think very
seriously of this boyish and silly publication."
As to the proposal of placing the children with
their mother's family: "We think it right to
say that Mr. Westbrook formerly kept a coffee-
house, and is certainly in no respect qualified
to be the guardian of Mr. Shelley's children.
To Miss Westbrook there are more decided
objections: she is illiterate and vulgar, and it
was by her advice, with her active concurrence,
and it may be said by her *management,* that Mr.
Shelley, when of the age of nineteen, ran away
with Miss Harriet Westbrook, then of the age
of seventeen, and married her in Scotland. Miss
Westbrook, the proposed guardian, was then
nearly thirty, and, if she had acted as she ought
to have done as the guardian and friend of her
younger sister, all this misery and disgrace to
both families would have been avoided."

His counsel's ingenious notion of winning his
client's case by renouncing in that client's name
the opinions of his youth, seemed to Shelley a
piece of disgusting hypocrisy. He, therefore,
drew up for the Lord Chancellor a statement in

which he set forth that his ideas on marriage had not changed, and that if he had made his conduct conform to the customs of society, he in no way had renounced the liberty to criticize those customs.

The Lord Chancellor in his judgment remarks: "This is a case in which a father has demonstrated that he must and does deem it to be a matter of duty to recommend to those whose opinions and habits he may take upon himself to form conduct as moral and virtuous, which the law calls upon me to consider as immoral and vicious. . . . I cannot, therefore, in these conditions, entrust him with the guardianship of these children."

But the Lord Chancellor refused to confide them to the odious Westbrooks. He put them under the care of an Army doctor, named Hume, of Brent End Lodge, Hanwell, who would place the boy, when seven years old, at a good private school under the superintendence of an orthodox clergyman. As to the little Ianthe, she would be brought up at home by Mrs. Hume, who would see that she had her morning prayers, and asked a blessing on her food. Mrs. Hume would also put into her hands improving books, and, to a certain extent, would encourage the reading of poetry, Shakespeare for instance, if carefully Bowdlerized. The whole cost, one hundred a year for each child. Mr. Shelley might visit them twelve times a year, but in the presence of Dr. and Mrs. Hume. Mr. John Westbrook might see them the same number of times, but, if he wished it, he might see them without the Humes being present.

This sentence was very bitter to Shelley. It sanctioned officially, so to say, and in reasonable and moderate formulas, his exile from the community of civilized men. It was like a brevet of incurable folly.

.   .   .   .

While the case was being fought out, he had bought a house in the pleasant little country town of Great Marlow. Ariel at last consented to have a home like other people. One room, big enough for a village ball-room, was fitted up as a library, and decorated with casts of Venus and Apollo. There was a very big garden: in this during the spring and summer of 1817 might be seen two babies, William and Clara Shelley, and a third child of unusual beauty, Allegra, daughter of Lord Byron and Claire. Her father was said to be leading a wild life at Venice. Claire received no news from him.

Shelley's recent trials had left their traces on his countenance. He was thinner, more hectic, and stooped more than ever. A violent pain in his side prevented him from sleeping, and the doctors, unable to cure it, said it was "a nervous disorder."

His state of mind was despondent. Life had brought him so much suffering, his good intentions had been repaid by such evil results, that he had taken a horror of every sort of action. He felt an intense but undefined desire to withdraw from the perilous throngs of men, men whose reactions cannot be predicted, and who are swayed by such terrible gusts of passion. The regeneration of the real world now appeared to him so unrealizable that he no longer sought satisfaction therein for his loves and hatreds, but looked for it in the more docile and malleable world of the imagination. Subjects for poems, vague and shadow-like, floated round him, which, feeding on his sorrowful thoughts, gradually took form at the expense of his powers of action.

The aërial edifices, the crystalline palaces, which with their filmy vapours had so long hidden from him the actual world, seemed to detach themselves from earth and to float up as though drawn by an invisible force. They did not melt away, but swaying with a gentle movement rose in all their translucent glory to the high realms of pure Poetry. In the place which

223

they had occupied, Shelley now saw the world
as it is, the brown earth arduous to cultivate,
the harsh faces of men, women full of nerves
and hysteria, the cruel and obstructive society
from which he longed to escape.

The poem which most often occupied his
thoughts was the story of an ideal Revolution.
He did not want the scenes of bloodshed which
ruined for him the otherwise inspiring story of
the French Revolution. He wanted his Revolution to be the work of a pair of lovers. His
personal experience had taught him that only
the love of a woman can inspire a sublime
courage.

Laon and Cythna, two ideal anarchists, were
to be the transfigured portraits of himself and
Mary. He would make them die at the stake,
for their ideas, as he would have liked to die
himself, exchanging a last kiss in the midst of
the flames, a kiss so delicious that the agony
would become a sort of voluptuous refinement
of ecstasy. For him love did not attain its maxi-
mum unless he could associate it with thoughts
and sufferings shared in common. Now that he
and Mary, married and fairly well off, seemed
about to begin an easier life, he desired to escape
from this somewhat commonplace happiness, and
to live in imagination the magnificent and peril-
224

ous destiny which might have been his in other lands and other ages.

He passed his time among the little islands of the Thames where the swans build their nests. Lying at the bottom of his boat completely hidden by the high grasses, he sought his inspiration in gazing up at the changing skies. The study of fleeting, interweaving colour and form had always given him immense pleasure, and every day he felt more strongly that his real mission in life was to seize the most transitory shades of beauty, and to fix them for ever in words buoyant and beautiful as themselves.

The entire summer was given to this entrancing work. Then he was obliged to go up to London. Money was getting scarce; he had so many mouths to feed. Besides Mary and the children, Claire and Allegra were dependent on him, and very often the entire Godwin household. His new friend, Leigh Hunt, with a wife and five children, needed help. He had promised Peacock a hundred a year so that he might go on writing his fine novels. Charles Clairmont, who was nothing to him, had fallen in love when in France with an ugly woman several years older than himself and of course penniless; it was Shelley who provided the means for marriage. Just as formerly, he had to go to the money-lenders in order to satisfy these endless claims. "You're a thoroughbred," Godwin once told him, "whom the horse-flies prevent from taking your spring."

Happily for him, Mary managed to bring him back to earth, and he forgave her, seeing her now only as the Cythna of his poem. But she, an over-anxious hostess, did not care for their too assiduous visitors, such as Peacock who dropped in every evening "without being asked," and drank up a whole bottle of wine. She wanted Shelley to find a purchaser for the Marlow house which they had bought too hastily. She saw he suffered from cold, and wished to take him away to a warmer climate, perhaps to Italy.

"Dearest love," she wrote to him in London. . . . "Pray in your letters do be more explicit! You have advertised the house but have you given Madocks any orders about how to answer applicants? And have you settled yet for Italy or the sea? And do you know how to get money to convey us there, and to buy the things that will be absolutely necessary before our departure? And can you do anything for my father before you go? Or, after all, would it not be as well to inhabit a small house by the seashore where our expenses would be much

226

less than they are at present? You have not yet mentioned to Godwin your thoughts of Italy; but if you determine soon, I would have you do it, as those things are always better to be talked of some days before they take place.

"I took my first walk to-day. What a dreadfully cold place this house is! I was shivering over a fire and the garden looked cold and dismal, but so soon as I got into the road I found to my infinite surprise that the sun was shining and the air warm and delightful.

"I wish Willy to be my companion in my future walks; to further which plan will you send down if possible by Monday's coach, a sealskin fur hat for him? It must be a fashionable round shape, *for a boy* mention particularly, and have a narrow gold ribbon round it, that it may be taken in if too large. . . . I am just now surrounded by babes. Allegra is scratching and crowing, William amusing himself with wrapping a shawl round him, and Miss Claire staring at the fire. . . . Adieu, dearest love! I want to say again that you may fully answer me, how very, very anxious I am to know the whole extent of your present difficulties and pursuits."

One source of annoyance to Mary was the

presence of Alba in the house. The neighbours had been told that she was the child of a lady in London and had been sent to the country for her health, but anyone could see from Claire's behaviour that the child was hers. The pure-minded jumped at once to the conclusion that Shelley was the father. The old accusations of promiscuity again reared their heads, and Mary's prudishness suffered from it. One of the reasons for which she wished to go to Italy was that the journey would enable them to take the little girl out to Lord Byron.

Shelley's one wish also was to depart. The ties of family, of friendship, of business, had raised round him intangible walls behind which he was stifling. His will was rock-like, but life's little waves, perfidious and unconcerned, ate away at it ceaselessly. In England where the highest legal dignity had taken from him his civic rights, he had the sensation of standing always in the pillory. It seemed to him that in flying from England, he would become again a free and aërial spirit, that in a new country his life would be like a sheet of white paper on which he could compose a new existence in the same way that he could compose a poem.

When their departure was fixed, Mary asked to have the children baptized. She thought it
228

was better for them to start in life by observing the Rules of the Game. Shelley agreed, and at the same time that William Shelley and Clara Everina Shelley were christened, Byron's daughter was christened too under the names of Clara Allegra.

CHAPTER XXVI

"QUEEN OF MARBLE AND OF MUD"

THE clear sky of Italy, the constant, cloud-less, sky. Once more the caravan of three went down towards the lands of forgetfulness and sunshine. The babies and nursemaids who this time went with it, were hardly any drag on its rapid and whimsical progress.

Milan was reached by way of the Mont Cenis, where the first halt was made to await news of Byron, to whom Shelley had written informing him of the arrival of his daughter. Shelley passed his days in the Cathedral reading the *Inferno* and *Purgatorio,* in a solitary spot behind the altar where the light of day beneath the storied window is yellow and dim. Churches no longer inspired in him the horror they used to do. He was surprised to find that since he had suffered so keenly no place now seemed to fit his feelings better or to be a finer background to the greatness of human passions than a church. In the company of Dante, and in the midst of

230

a symphony of warm, rich colours, the Catholic religion no longer seemed to be the invention of charlatans.

Byron's answer came. Nothing on earth would induce him to see Claire, and he would leave at once any town to which she should come. As to the child, he was willing to under-take the charge of its education, but his possession must be absolute. Shelley considered that this condition was cruel, and pleaded with Byron to soften it. But Byron, who above all things dreaded scenes with Claire, refused to cede an iota. A Venetian met in Milan gave tidings that the "English Lord" was leading a life of debauchery, and keeping a whole harem. Such news was hardly reassuring for Allegra's education, and Shelley begged Claire to give up all idea of help from Byron rather than let him have the child. As usual he undertook to pay for everything himself. But Claire, proud of Allegra's birth, wanted to obtain for her all the advantages of it. She had every confidence in Elise, the Swiss nurse who had brought the baby up, and she decided to send them both to Venice. In spite of Shelley's affectionate remonstrances Allegra was handed over to her father.

. . . .

Disquieting news of the child soon came to

trouble Claire. Byron had only kept it a few weeks. At first very proud of its beauty and of seeing it admired by the Venetians on the Piazza, he soon tired of this and allowed Mrs Hoppner, wife of the English Consul, to take charge of it. Who was this Mrs. Hoppner? Elise wrote that she was a very kind lady, but Claire began to suffer from terrible remorse. During a whole year she had never been parted from the child for a single hour. She adored it. Allegra was the only creature in the whole world she could call her very own, since her family renounced her, and her lover refused to see her. Shelley, unable to bear the sight of her misery, offered to go with her to Venice. Mary consented to the arrangement in spite of her dislike at seeing these two start on a journey together. Paolo, the servant, who was energetic and seemed reliable, went with them as courier. In order not to irritate Byron, who had forbidden Claire to enter any town where he might happen to be, it was decided that she should stop at Padua and wait there the upshot of Shelley's embassy. But finding herself so near to Allegra, she could not resist going on. She thought that by keeping her presence secret she could manage to see the child, and so she and Shelley took a gondola and went down the Brenta. They crossed the lagoon in the middle of the night, in a violent storm of wind, rain and lightning, while in the distance the lights of Venice shone dimly behind a curtain of mist.

The next morning they went to the Hoppners', who received them with courtesy and kindness. Mrs. Hoppner sent at once for Elise and the baby. She was much grown, was pale, and had lost a great deal of her liveliness, but was as beautiful as ever. Then they had a long conversation on the subject of Byron. The Hoppners, worthy people of conventional ideas, young lovers much excited by all the intrigues going on round them though humanized a little by Venetian indulgence, related with many head-shakes:

From the third day of his arrival Byron had provided himself, as he liked to boast, with a gondola and a mistress. The mistress was Marianna Segati, wife of a cloth-merchant, who was the poet's landlord, for he had let rooms to Byron in his house. A most imprudent proceeding, but the cloth-business was doing badly. Marianna was twenty-two, had splendid black eyes, and a delicious voice. Although belonging to the middle classes, she was received by the aristocracy of Venice on account of her singing. That she should lose her heart to the noble lord who was as generous as he was handsome, and who lived under the same roof, was as inevitable as are the simplest chemical reactions. As to the Merchant of Venice, Byron was free with his ducats, and Venetian morals always permitted *one* lover. Mrs. Hoppner, a friendly little woman with intelligent eyes, had told this story with that mixture of Christian sorrow and mundane relish which the virtuous employ in talking of the vicious. Her husband, with many hums and haws, added that this was not all. The Venetian populace circulated a tale that somewhere in the city the English Lord had a closed villa, in which, one Muse not sufficing him, he had gathered together the whole Nine. A legendary history was growing up concerning Byron, and the travelling British spoke with bated breath of Nero and Heliogabalus. The lower classes adored him, and at Carnival time the women took advantage of their masks and dominoes to hook themselves on to his person.

Such gossip was far from reassuring to Claire. She asked what ought she to do? The Consul advised her above all things not to let Byron suspect she was in Venice, for he often expressed his extreme horror of her arrival.

At three o'clock Shelley went to the Palazzo Mocenigo to call on Byron, who was delighted to see him, Shelley being perhaps the only man in the world with whom Byron would talk seriously and as crowned head to crowned head. Even when told of the reason for Shelley's journey, and Claire's great desire to see the child again, he remained calm and reasonable. He said he understood perfectly Claire's anxiety, but that he could not send Allegra back to her, because the Venetians, who already accused him of capriciousness, would say he had grown tired of her. However, he would think the matter over, and find some way to arrange everything. On which, he invited Shelley to go for a ride with him along the Lido.

The gondola took them across the lagoon, and they disembarked on the long, sandy island which defends Venice from the Adriatic. Nothing grows here but sea-wrack and thistle. They found Byron's horses waiting for them. Shelley loved all wild and solitary places, and this gallop along the edge of the sea was delightful to him. Only the knowledge that Claire, at the Hoppners', anxiously awaited his return, spoiled his pleasure.

Byron inveighed against the stupidity of the English. Those who came to Venice persecuted him with their curiosity, and even offered money to his servants to allow them to see his bedroom.

Then he spoke of Shelley's own misfortunes with many protestations of friendship. "Had I been in England at the time of the Chancery affair, I would have moved heaven and earth to get you back your children."

This led him on to speak of the wickedness of humanity which he judged to be infinite. "Men are filled with hatred of one another. To expect or hope for anything else is the mark of the visionary."

"Why?" asked Shelley. "You appear to believe that man is the victim of his instincts without being able to direct them. . . . My faith is quite different. I think that our will creates our virtue. . . . And though wickedness may be natural that does not prove it to be invincible."

Byron pointed out the patrician city that the setting sun suffused with gold and sombre purple. "Let us get into the gondola again," he said, "I want to show you something." When they had glided for some moments over the lagoon, "Look over to the west. Don't you hear the clang of a bell?"

Shelley looking, saw on a small island a windowless, deformed, and dreary building, and on the top of it an open tower in which a bell swung in black relief against the crimson sky.

236

With the splash of the oars seemed to mingle distant, stifled cries for help.

"That," Byron said, "is the madhouse. Every evening when I cross the water at this hour, I hear the bell clanging the maniacs to vespers."

"No doubt that they may thank the Creator for his mercy towards them?"

"Always the same Shelley!" laughed Byron. "Infidel and blasphemer! You who can't swim, beware of providence! But you spoke just now of vanquishing our instincts. Does it not seem to you that this spectacle rather is an image of our life? Conscience is the bell that calls us to virtue. We obey it like the madmen without knowing why. Then the sun sets, the bell stops, it is the night of death."

He looked towards Venice, which, huddled in the twilight, had become a rose-tinged grey.

"We Byrons," said he, "die young . . . on my father's side, and on my mother's as well. . . . It's all the same to me, but I intend first to enjoy my youth."

.   .   .   .

The next day Shelley, who had come to Byron filled with forebodings, was agreeably surprised to find him quite reasonable. He offered to lend Shelley and Claire for two months a villa he owned at Este, and to allow Allegra to go and stay there with her mother. Shelley joyfully accepted this generous offer, and he wrote to Mary to come at once and join them:

"I have been obliged to decide on all these things without you. I have done for the best; and, my own beloved Mary, you must soon come and scold me if I have done wrong, and kiss me if I have done right, for I am sure I do not know which, and it is only the event that will show. We shall at least be saved the trouble of introduction, and have formed acquaintance with a lady (Mrs. Hoppner) who is so good, so beautiful, so angelically sweet that, were she as wise, too, she would be quite a Mary, but she is not very accomplished. Her eyes are like a reflection of yours; her manners are like yours when you know and like a person. . . . Kiss the blue-eyed darlings for me, and do not let Willmouse forget me. Ca cannot recollect me."

Mary's journey was slow and disagreeable. At Florence she was held up by passport difficulties. The baby Clara, who was cutting her teeth, suffered from heat, fatigue and the change of milk; when Este was reached, she was dangerously ill.

During fourteen days she remained in a state

of fever. The doctor seemed a stupid fellow, and Mary decided to go on to Venice that she might call in a better one. At Fusina the Austrian custom-house officers stopped them and attempted to prevent them from crossing the lagoon Shelley, who had gone to meet them at Padua, insisted with extraordinary violence on passing, and rushed for a gondola. The baby had curious convulsive twitchings of the eyes and mouth. During the voyage she was almost unconscious. When the hotel was reached her condition was still more alarming. Examined by a doctor, he said at once there was no hope. Within an hour she died silently and without pain.

Mary found herself standing in the hall of a strange inn with her dead child in her arms. Mr. Hoppner came and took her and Shelley away to his own house. The next morning Shelley carried the little corpse in a gondola for burial on the Lido, and Mary tried to shake off her grief. It was one of Godwin's doctrines that only weak and cowardly natures abandon themselves to sorrow, which could not last did we not feed it in secret by finding a sort of painful vanity in our suffering. His daughter shared his ideas on this point. The day after little Ca was buried, she wrote in her journal:

"*Sunday, September* 27. Read fourth canto of *Childe Harold.* It rains. Go to the Doge's Palace, Ponte dei Sospiri, etc. Go to the Academy with Mr. and Mrs. Hoppner, and see some fine pictures, call at Lord Byron's, and see the Fornarina."

.   .   :   .   .   .   .

The Fornarina was Byron's latest mistress, a peasant woman with a face of the fine antique Venetian type. "You will see how beautiful she is," Byron had told Shelley. "Very fine black eyes and the figure of a Juno, wavy black hair which reflects the moonlight; one of those women who would go to hell for love. I like that sort of animal, and I should certainly have preferred Medea to any other woman in the world."

Certainly this beautiful baker's wife was a strange sort of animal, and quite untamable. She was so fierce that all the servants were terrified of her, even Tita, the gigantic gondolier. She was jealous, insupportable, and false as the devil, besides being perfectly ridiculous from the moment she had insisted on replacing her veil and shawl by fashionable gowns and hats with ostrich feathers. Byron flung these into the fire every time he saw them, and then she went out and bought others. But he put up with her

240

follies because she amused him. He liked her
vivacity, her Venetian dialect, her violence. Her
coarse and animal nature was, he imagined, more
of a rest to him than anything else after intellectual labour. Thanks to her his poem advanced
with a splendid motion, with something of the
wild and natural movement of the sea or the
passionate love of a woman.

To the Shelleys, who were ultra-refined, this
magnificent animal was highly displeasing. They
exchanged sorrowful glances. During the few
days they spent in Venice, Shelley became better
acquainted with Byron's mode of life and he
judged it with severity. The Poet admitted to
his orgies the lowest women picked up by his
gondolieri in the streets. Then, despising himself, he decreed that man is despicable. His
cynicism now appeared to Shelley to be nothing
but a graceful mask for his sensuality.

At length the Shelleys went back to Este,
depressed by their return there without their
little girl. Yet the house was cheerful. In the
garden a vine-covered pergola led to a summer-
house which Shelley made his study. From
thence you saw the ruins of the ancient castle of
Este in the foreground, then, like a green sea,
Lombardy's waveless plains, on which cities and
villages seemed like islands bounded by vaporous

air . . . in the distance many-domed Padua, a peopled solitude, and the towers of Venice glittered in the sunshine against a sapphire sky.

He worked hard. He had begun *Prometheus Unbound,* a lyrical drama on the Book of Job. He tried to fix in verse light as wing-beats the melancholy beauty of these autumn days. But no sooner had the intoxicating joy of composition faded, than he felt himself once more alone and forgotten. It seemed to him that in the frail bark which carried beneath an alien sky his group of youthful exiles Misery stood at the helm.

CHAPTER XXVII

THE ROMAN CEMETERY

AT the end of another month the villa must again be given up to Byron and Allegra restored to him. The cold and rainy weather gave Shelley the idea of pushing further south. To feel happy he needed warmth and sympathy. New climates and new places might cheat his sorrow.

The road to Rome wound along among already-reddening vineyards. At every step the travellers passed teams of cream-coloured oxen of Virgilian beauty. They went through Ferrar and Bologna, where they saw such quantities of statues, pictures and churches that Shelley's brain became like the portfolio of an architect or a print-shop or a commonplace book. Passing by the romantic cities of Rimini, Spoleto and Terni, they reached the Campagna di Roma, an absolute solitude yet picturesque and charming. When they entered Rome an immense hawk was sailing in the air over their heads.

The majestic ruins of Rome impressed Shelley tremendously. The English burying-place, under the pyramidal tomb of Cestius, appeared to him the most beautiful and solemn cemetery he had ever seen. The wind made the leaves sing in the trees above the graves of young girls and of little children. In such a place one might have hoped to sleep.

From Rome they went on to Naples, where they took rooms which looked across the Villa Nazionali to the blue waters of the bay, for ever changing and for ever the same. Night and day they saw Vesuvius smoking, and the reflection of its flames, and its shadow in the sea. The climate was that of an English spring, though lacking a little that crescendo of sweetness which delights one in England when April's there.

They went to Pompeii, to Salerno, to Pæstum, getting exquisite but transitory glimpses, that leave in the memory dim white visions as of some half-remembered dream. But, in spite of all this beauty, they were not happy. They knew no one and their perpetual loneliness was hard to bear.

Basking in the splendid Italian sunshine they thought with longing of Windsor, of Marlow, even of London. What was the use of all these mountains, of all this blue sky without any friends? Social enjoyment, in some form or other, is the Alpha and Omega of existence, and, no matter how real or how beautiful the actual landscape may be, it vanishes into smoke in the mind when one thinks of some familiar forms of scenery, commonplace perhaps in themselves, but over which old memories throw a delightful hue.

In the streets they looked with envy at the workmen and even at the beggars with whom other workmen and other beggars passed the time of day. Shelley, who felt himself so full of affection for mankind, was painfully surprised to find himself always alone in the midst of multitudes. Mary disliked particularly being "a foreigner" wherever she went. She was at the beginning of a new pregnancy; Claire got on her nerves insupportably. She had serious domestic troubles. The Italian valet, Paolo, had seduced the Swiss nurse. Mary insisted he should marry her, and when at last he consented to do so, it was to take his departure immediately with his wife, vowing vengeance against Shelley. Next Claire fell ill of a mysterious malady which Mary misunderstood.

Discontented and tired of Naples they decided to return to Rome. A need of constant change ate up their tranquillity; they were like a sick man who for ever seeks a fresher, cooled place in the bed, and seeks in vain since he takes with him his fever wherever he moves. The heat of the southern spring had tired the little boy, "Willmouse," his father's darling. The doctor advised them to take him northwards immediately to Lucca. They were on the point of starting when he was seized with a violent attack of dysentery.

During sixty hours, Shelley held the child's hand in his; he loved him more and more. Willie was an affectionate, intelligent and sensitive child. He had beautiful hair, fair and silky, a transparent complexion, Shelley's eyes, blue and animated. While he slept the Italian maids would come on tiptoe into the room to point him out one to the other. Already in the convulsions of death, the doctor still hoped to save him. He lived three days longer and then died at noon on a day of gorgeous sunshine. He was buried in the Protestant cemetery which on his first visit to Rome had so impressed Shelley by its loveliness and solemn seclusion. The wind was still whispering in the leaves of the trees.

Near an ancient tomb in the sunny flower-starred grass, Shelley saw his dead child disappear.

Fanny . . . Harriet . . . Baby Clara . . . William . . . It seemed to him that he was surrounded by a pestilential atmosphere which infected one after the other all those he had loved best.

. . . .

The young couple, whom the gods thus amused themselves in persecuting, had, so far, bravely borne the blows. But now Mary gave up the struggle. Shelley took her away to a pleasant villa in the country, but she was indifferent to everything. Always she saw little feet running over the sands at Naples, heard delicious childish phrases expressing mingled love and glee. Motionless, gazing away in a sort of torpor, she only roused herself to talk of the tomb in Rome. She wanted for her beautiful boy a block of white marble, and flowers.

Godwin, hearing of her condition, and using "the privilege of a father and a philosopher," expostulated with her. She was putting herself quite among "the commonalty and mob of her sex." What did she need that she had not? She possessed the husband of her choice, and all the goods of fortune, and thereby the means of being useful to others. "But you have lost a child, and

247

all the rest of the world, and all that is beautiful, and all that has a claim upon your kindness is nothing, because a child of three years old is dead!"

Shelley himself gently complained:

> My dearest Mary, wherefore hast thou gone,
> And left me in this dreary world alone?
> Thy form is here indeed—a lovely one—
> But *thou* art fled, gone down the dreary road
> That leads to Sorrow's most obscure abode.

As for him, he had his aërial refuges, and once safely shut therein the lugubrious tragedies of his life seemed like absurd nightmares. He occupied himself with *Prometheus,* a new presentation of the one and only theme of his genius: the war of the Spirit against Matter, the war of Free Man against the World. In it Jupiter becomes a sort of Lord Castlereagh, the Titan another Shelley, a victim filled with hope and confident in the ultimate triumph of Good. The cloudless skies, the eddyings of the wild west wind, each and all were a pretext for singing his faith filled with the optimism of despair, a faith no misfortune could quell.

When the moment for Mary's confinement was near, they went on to Florence, in order to be within reach of a good doctor. But the best doctor was Florence herself, a city in which solitude has no bitterness. At Florence one lives with Dante; one sits by the side of Savonarola; one watches Giotto pass by. In the churches Brunelleschi and Donatello are still in friendly rivalry. The statues in the streets live with a more intense life than anywhere else. On the Piazza di San Miniato, Michael Angelo's *David* triumphantly challenges Bandinelli's silly *Neptune* and clumsy *Hercules*. One suffers less from not knowing the children who play near one, because one possesses the children of Della Robbia.

From the hill of San Miniato Shelley loved to gaze over the city. The red roofs stood out sharply, the Arno rolled its yellow, rain-swollen waters between the old houses, which seemed to huddle along the quays and bridges like a crowd of human beings; in the distance the valley touched a horizon of bluish hills.

In the intellectual atmosphere of Florence, Mary began to take a new interest in life. At the boarding-house she "mixed a little with the people downstairs." She got through the birth-time quickly and well. When once more she found herself with a baby in her arms, she smiled for the first time since the death of William.

She had her son christened Percy Florence.

CHAPTER XXVIII

"ANY WIFE TO ANY HUSBAND"

EVERYTHING in life comes in series. One friend brings another. Mary and Percy, after suffering so much from loneliness, suddenly found themselves, without having sought it, the centre of a gay and pleasant circle.

Chance had worked the miracle. First of all Shelley had begun to suffer again from the pain in his side. The wind from the Apennines, so boisterous in Florence during the winter, tried him greatly, and the doctor recommended Pisa as more sheltered.

Tom Medwin, one of his cousins, came to join him there. Medwin had been in a dragoon regiment in India, from which he was now retired with the rank of Captain. He had literary aspirations, and on this account sought the society of the only literary member of the family. He was a good fellow, though a deadly bore, but he introduced to the Shelleys a charming couple, the Williamses.

"ANY WIFE TO ANY HUSBAND"

Edward Williams, after three years in the Navy, had exchanged from that branch of the service into the 8th Dragoon Guards, then quartered in India, where he had made Medwin's acquaintance. He had been obliged to sell out, he always explained, because of his health. Frank, fearless, with no pretensions, and interested in everything, the Shelleys liked him extremely, and they found his wife charming. She was a very pretty woman with much sweetness of manner, and an excellent musician. The two couples became great friends and at last the Shelleys knew the delights of informal visiting, of ungrudging admiration and praise, and of the perfect confidence which makes the joy of any real friendship.

The moment a social circle exists it attracts to its centre all the lonely souls drifting round its circumference. Thus, came Taaffe, the Irish count; Mavrocordato, the Greek prince; and an extraordinary Italian priest with the diabolic and piercing eye of a Venetian inquisitor. This was the reverend professor, Pacchiani, known as the Devil of Pisa, abbé without religion, professor without a chair, amateur of women and pictures, antiquary, pimp, dilettante, and go-between in general.

Always with some *palazzo* or other to let, he

would take his commission from the tenant as well as from the landlord; he would warmly recommend a teacher of Italian, and divide with him the price paid for the lessons; to the rich Englishman passing through Venice he would give, in strictest confidence, the address of a *marquese* wishing to sell an Andrea del Sarto.

On familiar terms in every house the moment he had got his foot within the door, he called Mary and her friend Jane, "le belle Inglese," and amused them by telling them tales of the great ladies of Pisa, to whom he was father confessor and tame cat.

   .   .   .   .

One of Pacchiani's stories made a deep impression on Shelley. Count Viviani, a great Florentine nobleman, had just married, for the second time, a woman much younger than himself. By his first wife he had two lovely daughters, and the new countess, jealous of their beauty, had persuaded her husband to send them to Pisa and shut them up each in a separate convent, until husbands were found who would take them without dowries. The professor, who had known the *contessine* since their childhood, spoke with enthusiasm of their wit and beauty. The eldest in particular was almost a genius.

"Poverina!" said Pacchiani. "She pines like

a bird in a cage. She sees her youth slipping away unused, and she is made for love. Yesterday she was watering some flowers in her cell—she has nothing else to love but her flowers—'Yes,' she told them, 'you were born to vegetate, but we, thinking beings, we were created for action and not to wither away in one place. . . .' A miserable place too is that convent of St. Anna; at this moment the poor inmates are shivering with cold, being allowed nothing to warm them but a few ashes which they carry about in an earthen vase. You would pity them."

This story re-awoke in Shelley all his instincts of knight-errantry, which the comforts of conjugal life had stilled during recent years. He asked dozens of questions, and showed such hot indignation with the Count, such interest in the fair victim, that Pacchiani could not resist the pleasure—always delicious to an old man of his sort—of bringing two young people together. He offered to take Shelley to the convent of St. Anna.

It was in all conscience a miserable place, a ruinous building situated in an unfrequented street in the suburbs. The visitors crossed a gloomy portal and the abbé went to find Emilia. Mephistopheles came back accompanied by Gretchen. He had not exaggerated her beauty. Her

253

black hair was tied in a simple knot, after the manner of a Greek Muse. Her faultless contour seemed the work of Praxiteles: the marble-like pallor of her skin made more resplendent her large black eyes, full of a sleepy voluptuousness, in which certain Italian women surpass even Orientals.

The moment she appeared in the sombre parlour, Shelley felt that he loved her, and love with him was no desire of the flesh, but a need for self-sacrifice to that which he adored. Ever at the back of his mind dwelt his ideal of perfect physical beauty united to perfect spiritual beauty, the myth of a lovely and persecuted woman whose knight he would become, some Andromeda to whom he would play Perseus, some Princess for whom he would be St. George; a myth which had always been the motive of his love adventures, which had led him to run away with Harriet to save her from her father, and to love Mary because she was unhappy. It was a sentiment made up in proportions unknown to himself, of desire and pity, which, earthy perhaps in the beginning, had been so purified that it now merely raised to the highest point his creative power in poetry.

In Mary he had long believed this mystic love had been found. She fell indeed as little short of

a goddess as any woman may do. For the first
time, perhaps, the real woman coincided with
the Shelleyan image of her. Nevertheless, daily
life with her had shown him traits quite incompatible with divinity. Mary, mother of a family
and housekeeper, was a drier, a more practical
Mary, than the loving and courageous young
girl of Skinner Street. What Shelley had been
used to praise as her diamond-like purity, now
seemed to him to partake of the coldness of ice,
while her jealousy had become inconceivably
petty. Worst of all, he now knew her too inti-
mately to be able any longer to find in her a
quickening of his ideas.

In the beautiful and mysterious Emilia, on the
contrary, he could incarnate his whole soul, because he knew nothing about her. At long last,
he discovered in this Italian convent the adorable and fleeting vision which he had pursued
since boyhood, and which, every time that he
had thought to seize it, had vanished away, leaving him in presence of a flesh-and-blood woman
capable of wounding his sensitive soul.

On coming into the parlour, Emilia addressed
herself to a caged bird in terms which appeared
to Shelley the most poetic in the world:

"Poor little bird, you are dying of languor!
How I pity you! How much you must suffer

255

hearing the other birds calling to you, ere they
depart for warmer climes! But you are doomed,
like me, to finish in this prison your miserable
life. . . . Ah, why can I not free you!"

She was fond of improvising thus in Italian
fashion all sorts of spoken poems that did not
fail in quality—nor in quantity either. But Shelley saw in her true genius. He begged leave to
come and call upon her again and to bring with
him his wife and his sister-in-law. She graciously
gave her permission.

When he described the visit to Mary, he made
no secret of the sentiments with which it had
inspired him. Both of them were great readers
of Plato, and Mary was familiar with that love
which is merely the contemplation of supreme
beauty. She would, however, have been better
pleased to see it awakened by a statue, or that
Shelley, like Dante, had never had the chance of
speaking to his Beatrice. However, when Shelley begged her to go with him to see the beautiful
prisoner, she willingly went.

She admitted that Emilia was beautiful in a
Greek statue style, and of surprising eloquence,
but at the bottom of her heart she felt that she
preferred the chaste reserve of the viaggetory
Englishwoman to this too effusive Italian genius.
She thought that Emilia's voice was over loud,
256

that her gestures, if expressive, were wanting in grace, and that she was most agreeable when she held her tongue—which was seldom. However, Mary was careful not to let her real sentiments appear on the surface; on the contrary she expressed for Emilia the warmest friendship.

Claire, more impressionable than Mary, fell, like Shelley, an immediate victim to Emilia's charms. While Mary took the prisoner little presents, books, a gold chain, Claire, who was poor, offered the only thing she could give, namely, lessons in English. Emilia accepted with joy. An endless correspondence began between the convent and Pisa, and it was nothing but "Dear Sister!" "Adored Mary!" *"Sensible Percy! . . . Caro fratello!"* and even, in a mystic sense needless to say, *"Adorato sposo!"* Strangely enough, "dear sister Mary" sometimes showed a slight coldness. "But your husband tells me that this apparent coldness is only the ashes which cover an affectionate heart."

The truth is, that Emilia was beginning to get on dear sister Mary's nerves, for Shelley was busy in raising round her one of those aërial worlds into which he loved to escape. He was writing, in her honour, a magnificent love-poem, which he intended to make as mysterious as

ARIEL

Dante's *Vita Nuova*, or the *Sonnets* of Shakespeare.

> I never was attached to that great sect,
> Whose doctrine is that each one should select
> Out of the crowd a mistress or a friend,
> And all the rest, though fair and wise commend
> To cold oblivion, though it is in the code
> Of modern morals, and the beaten road
> Which those poor slaves with weary footsteps tread,
> Who travel to their home among the dead
> By the broad highway of the world, and so
> With one chained friend, perhaps a jealous foe
> The dreariest and the longest journey go.
> True love in this differs from gold and clay
> That to divide is not to take away.
> Love is like understanding that grows bright,
> Gazing on many truths: 'tis like thy light
> Imagination! . . .
>   Narrow
> The heart that loves, the brain that contemplates. . . .
> One object, and one form.

He drew a picture of Emilia which was one long pæan to her beauty:

> Warm fragrance seems to fall from her light dress
> And her loose hair: and where some heavy tress
> The air of her own speed has disentwined,
> The sweetness seems to satiate the faint wind.
>
>   The brightness
> Of her divinest presence trembles through
> Her limbs, as underneath a cloud of dew

258

"ANY WIFE TO ANY HUSBAND"

Embodied in the windless heaven of June,
Amid the splendour of winged stars, the Moon
Burns inextinguishably beautiful.

Spouse! Sister! Angel! Pilot of the Fate
Whose course has been so starless! O too late
Beloved! O too soon adored by me!
                                        Emily
A ship is floating in the harbour now. . . .

It was the most impassioned of invitations to set
sail for some lovely and impossible Elysian isle.
There

We shall become the same, we shall be one
Spirit within two frames, oh! wherefore two? . . .
Our breath shall intermix, our bosoms bound,
And our veins beat together. . . .
One hope within two wills, one will beneath
Two overshadowing minds, one life, one death,
One heaven, one hell, one immortality,
And one annihilation. Woe is me!
The winged words on which my soul would pierce
Into the height of Love's rare Universe,
Are chains of lead around its flight of fire——
I pant, I sink, I tremble, I expire!

Although Mary consoled herself by repeating
that all these fine phrases were addressed to the
divine essence of Emilia and not to a very pretty
girl with black eyes and black tresses, yet, at the
same time, it was vexing to see Shelley writing
with such enthusiasm. Happily, he was so en-

259

grossed by the ardour of composition that he had no time to go and see the poem's heroine. And while her platonic lover multiplied his aërial metaphors, Emilia received from the Count, her father, a cynical message. He had found a husband who would take her without a penny, and he requested her to let him know whether she accepted. The gentleman in question, a certain Biondi, was not attractive, and he inhabited a distant castle, surrounded by swamps. Emilia had never seen him, nor was she to see him before the wedding-day. Such Turkish customs were supremely disgusting, yet what could she do? The Elfin king, married to a very real Mary, could not, evidently, free her from her dungeon. Were she to marry Biondi, this might be perhaps the beginning of a happier life. And if she didn't like the man, she would meet others she might like, for *cavalieri serventi* are to be found even in the midst of a swamp.

Shelley had not finished his poem before he learnt that Emilia was married.

. . . .

Six months later Mary wrote to a friend:

"Emilia has married Biondi; we hear that she leads him and his mother—to use a vulgarism—a devil of a life. The conclusion of our friendship, *a la Italiana,* puts me in mind of a nursery rhyme which runs thus:

> 'As I was going down Cranbourne Lane
>   Cranbourne Lane was dirty
> And there I met a pretty maid
>   Who dropt to me a curtsy.
> I gave her cakes, I gave her wine,
>   I gave her sugar-candy;
> But oh! the little naughty girl,
>   She asked me for some brandy.'

"Now turn 'Cranbourne Lane' into Pisan acquaintances, which I am sure are dirty enough, and 'brandy' into the wherewithal to buy brandy, and you have the whole story of Shelley's Italian Platonics."

And Shelley added: "I cannot look at my poem! The person whom it celebrates was a cloud instead of a Juno. . . . I think one is always in love with something or other; the error—and I confess it is not easy for spirits cased in flesh and blood to avoid it—consists in seeking in a mortal image the likeness of what is, perhaps, eternal."

CHAPTER XXIX

THE CAVALIERE SERVENTE

DURING the early days which followed her departure from Venice, Claire had received news of Allegra fairly often through the Hoppners. The child suffered from the cold. She had become quiet and grave as a little old woman. Mr. Hoppner thought it would be better to remove her from Venice. But it was impossible to have a conversation to any purpose with her father, who was sinking deeper and deeper into debauchery.

Some months went by without any news. Claire, very anxious, wrote letter after letter to the Hoppners, who did not reply. Then she learnt that a great change had taken place in Byron's existence. It had begun by his being seriously ill and obliged to keep his bed. Hoppner, who came to chat with him, had told him that his love affairs, far from scandalizing the Venetians any longer as he believed and hoped, now merely amused the *conversazioni* at his expense. He was spoken of as the prey of artful trollops who stole from him, tricked him, and then made fun of him in their Venetian dialect. Don Juan fell into a red-hot rage, and instantly all the priestesses of the Palazzo Mocenigo were turned out of doors, and sent back, each to her midden.

The moment he was well, he was seen again at the Venetian receptions, which he had so long forsaken. Thus he met the beauty of the season, a lovely blonde, seventeen years of age, just married to a noble grey-beard, the Count Guiccioli. The Pilgrim admired the lady's figure, her bust and arms in particular. The very first day he slipped into her hand, as he took leave, a note which she adroitly concealed. It was an assignation. She came. He who said he adored her was a great Poet, young, handsome, highly-born, and rich. Though surrounded by all that makes life desirable, she instantly gave herself to him without a struggle.

A few days later, the Count took his wife to Ravenna, and Teresa begged Byron to go too. "The charmer forgets that a man may be whistled anywhere *before,* but that *after*—a journey in an Italian June is a conscription, and therefore she should have been less liberal in Venice, or less exigent at Ravenna." The notion of romantic and constant love was odious to him. He did not budge, and was rather proud of his strength of mind.

From Ravenna she wrote again that she was very ill, and, where an appeal to love had failed, an appeal to pity succeeded. Don Juan set off, but not without stopping at Ferrara and other towns on the way, to sample the local beauties. Although making a show of indifference and even of boredom, he was very glad to join Teresa. Intelligent women such as Lady Byron or Claire got on his nerves: he had too great a contempt for the sex to ask from a mistress intellectual companionship. The bakers' wives and other wantons of Venice were of a species too far below him. But the Countess Guiccioli united a restful and affectionate stupidity with the elegance of a well-born woman. She kept and held without too much trouble this Everlasting Rover. Don Juan now played the part of a faithful and devoted sick-nurse. "Were I to lose her," he wrote, "I should lose a being who has run great risks for my sake, and whom I have every reason to love—but I must not think this possible. I do not know what I *should* do were she to die, but I ought to blow my brains out, and I hope that I should."

When his conquering Conquest had to leave

Ravenna for Bologna, he followed. He had become the classic *cicesbeo:* "But I can't say I don't feel the degradation of it. Better to be an unskilful Planter, an awkward settler, better to be a hunter, or anything, than a flatterer of fiddlers and fan carrier of a woman . . . and now I am *cavalier' sirvente!* By the holy! It's a strange sensation."

· · · · · · ·

Claire was told all this story, and that Byron had sent orders for Allegra to be brought to Bologna. The idea that her child was to live in the house of Byron's new mistress, who would have no reasons for loving her and possibly some for hating her, terrified Claire. She wrote a passionate letter asking to have her back. Byron replied:

"I disapprove so completely of the way children are brought up in the Shelley household that I should think in sending my daughter to you I was sending her into a hospital. Is it not so? Have they *reared* one?—Either she will go to England or I shall put her into a convent. But the child shall not quit me again to perish of starvation and green fruit, or be taught to believe that there is no Deity."

On receiving this letter, Claire notes in her caustic way: "Letter from Albé concerning green fruit and God"; but she wept over it too. Allegra in a convent of Italian nuns, who have no notion of cleanliness and no love for children, seemed to her a frightful idea. She sent despairful, violent, almost insolent letters to Byron, who wrote to complain of her to Shelley, and to inform him that for the future he should refuse all correspondence with her.

"I have no conception," Shelley answered, "of what Claire's letters to you contain, and but an imperfect one on the subject of her correspondence with you at all. One or two of her letters, but not lately, I have indeed seen; but as I thought them extremely childish and absurd, I requested her not to send them, and she afterwards told me she had written and sent others in the place of them. I cannot tell if those which I saw on that occasion were sent you or not. I wonder, however, at your being provoked at what Claire writes, though that she should write what is provoking is very probable. You are conscious of performing your duty to Allegra, and your refusal to allow her to visit Claire at this distance you consider to be part of that duty. That Claire should wish to see her is natural.

That her disappointment should vex her, and her vexation make her write absurdly is all in the usual order of things. But, poor thing, she is very unhappy and in bad health, and she ought to be treated with as much indulgence as possible. The weak and the foolish are in this respect the kings—they can do no wrong."

.   .   .   .

He himself had need of a similar loftiness of soul, to rise above the women's quarrels which distracted his household. Mary grew more and more short-tempered. Godwin overwhelmed her with requests for money, to which Shelley had decided no longer to reply. He had already given her father nearly five thousand pounds without any results and had gained, at this high price, a chastened wisdom and a painful knowledge of Godwin's ugly soul. As the bitter reproaches which the Philosopher now showered on Mary turned her milk, Shelley informed him that for the future he would intercept and suppress all letters likely to upset her: "Mary has not, nor ought she to have the disposal of money. If she had, poor thing, she would give it all to you. Such a father—I mean a man of such high genius—can be at no loss to find subjects on which to address such a daughter. . . . I need not tell you that the neglecting entirely to write

267

to your daughter from the moment that nothing could be gained by it, would admit of but one interpretation."

Mary, worried about her father, Claire, worried about her child, got terribly on each other's nerves, and their common admiration for the only man of the household was far more an obstacle to a good understanding than a help. Mary did all she knew to make Claire perceive she was unwanted, and once more Claire as before had to recognize it. An old lady of the English colony found her a place as governess in Florence, so she went away.

Shelley wrote her long and loving letters, but though these were quite innocent he did not show them to Mary, and he asked Claire not to mention them when she wrote to her sister, although such a want of frankness was little to his taste. His early conception of love had been of a unity of ideas and actions so perfect that any explanation was quite uncalled for between lovers. But life had taught him that perfection is not to be had, and something short of it must be accepted. There are certain persons for whom pure Truth is a poison. Mary could not take it except in very diluted doses.

CHAPTER XXX

A SCANDALOUS LETTER

ON the 16th September, 1820, R. B. Hoppner wrote from Venice to Lord Byron:

"MY DEAR LORD,

". . . You are surprised and with reason, at the change of my opinion respecting Shiloh; it certainly is not that which I once entertained of him; but if I disclose to you my fearful secret, I trust, for his unfortunate wife's sake, if not out of regard to Mrs. Hoppner and me, that you will not let the Shelleys know that we are acquainted with it. This request you will find so reasonable that I am sure you will comply with it, and I therefore proceed to divulge to you what indeed on Allegra's account it is necessary that you should know, as it will fortify you in the good resolution you have already taken never to trust her again to her mother's care.

"You must know then that at the time the Shelleys were here Claire was with child by Shel-

269

ley: you may remember to have heard that she was constantly unwell, and under the care of a Physician, and I am uncharitable enough to believe that the quantity of medicine she then took was not for the mere purpose of restoring her health. I perceive too why she preferred remaining alone at Este, notwithstanding her fear of ghosts and robbers, to being here with the Shelleys.

"Be this at it may, they proceeded from here to Naples where one night Shelley was called up to see Claire who was very ill. His wife, naturally, thought it very strange that he should be sent for; but although she was not aware of the nature of the connection between them she had had sufficient proof of Shelley's indifference, and of Claire's hatred for her: besides as Shelley desired her to remain quiet she did not dare to interfere.

"A Mid-wife was sent for, and the worthy pair, who had made no preparation for the reception of the unfortunate being she was bringing into the world, bribed the woman to carry it to the Pieta, where the child was taken half an hour after its birth, being obliged likewise to purchase the physician's silence with a considerable sum. During all the time of her confinement Mrs. Shelley, who expressed great anxiety on her account, was not allowed to approach her, and these beasts, instead of requiting her uneasiness on Claire's account by at least a few expressions of kindness, have since increased in their hatred of her, behaving to her in the most brutal manner, and Claire doing everything she can to engage her husband to abandon her.

"Poor Mrs. Shelley, whatever suspicions she may entertain of the nature of their connection, knows nothing of their adventure at Naples, and as the knowledge of it could only add to her misery, 'tis as well that she should not. This account we had from Elise, who passed here this summer with an English lady who spoke very highly of her. She likewise told us that Claire does not scruple to tell Mrs. Shelley that she wishes her dead, and to say to Shelley in her presence that she wonders how he can live with such a creature. . . .

"I think after this account you will no longer wonder that I have a bad opinion of Shelley. His talents I acknowledge but I cannot concur that a man can be as you say 'crazy against morality' and have honour. I have heard of honour among thieves, but there it means only interest, and though it may be to Shelley's interest to cut as respectable a figure as he can with the opinions he publicly professes, it is clear to me that honour does not direct any one of his actions.

"I fear my letter is written in a very incoherent style, but as I really cannot bring myself to go over this disgusting subject a second time; hope you will endeavour to comprehend it as it stands. . . .

"Adieu, my dear Lord, Believe me, Ever your——faithful Servant,

"R. B. HOPPNER."

Byron to Hoppner

"MY DEAR HOPPNER,

"Your letters and papers came very safely, though slowly, missing one post. The Shiloh story is true no doubt though Elise is but a sort of *Queen's evidence*. You remember how eager she was to return to them, and then she goes away and abuses them. Of the facts, however, there can be little doubt; it is just like them. You may be sure that I keep your counsel.

"Yours ever and truly,

"BYRON."

CHAPTER XXXI

LORD BYRON'S SILENCE

SHELLEY, invited by Lord Byron to come to Ravenna so that they might discuss important matters, found the Pilgrim in brilliant fettle. He looked in splendid health; for the reign of the Guiccioli had rescued him from the degrading libertinage of Venice. Fletcher himself had grown fatter, as the shadow increases in proportion with the body which throws it.

The Palazzo Guiccioli was a splendid affair, the household mounted on a royal scale. On the marble staircase Shelley met with every kind of animal making himself at home. Eight enormous dogs, three monkeys, five cats, an eagle, a parrot, and a falcon quarrelled together and made it up as it suited them. There were ten horses in the stables.

Byron welcomed him with great friendliness, and the night was passed in reading and discussing Byron's poems. The new cantos of *Don Juan* appeared admirable to Shelley. His contact with Byron's genius always reduced him to despair. Beside the solid structure of Byron's verse, his own seemed strangely fragile. He told Byron he ought to write a poem which would be for his time what the *Iliad* was for the Greeks. But Byron affected to despise posterity, and to take no interest in poetry except at a thousand guineas the canto.

Once again Shelley, the Ascetic, was obliged to adapt himself to the habits and customs of Byron the Magnificent. They got up at midday, they breakfasted at two, and worked until six in the evening. They rode from six to eight, dined, and spent the night talking until six o'clock next morning.

Byron did not talk merely of poetry. From the very first day, and with the most friendly air in the world, he posted Shelley up in the scandalous stories circulating about him amongst the English in Italy. In spite of having promised the Hoppners not to give them away, he showed Shelley the letter containing the calumnies of Elise. He declared, of course, that he had never given the smallest credence to the ridiculous tale, but that the Hoppners should have been so ready to believe it was, to Shelley, a heart-breaking blow. He wrote immediately to Mary.

274

LORD BYRON'S SILENCE

Shelley to Mary Shelley

"RAVENNA, *Aug.* 7, 1821.

"Lord Byron has told me of a circumstance that shocks me exceedingly, because it exhibits a degree of desperate and wicked malice, for which I am at a loss to account. When I hear such things, my patience and my philosophy are put to a severe proof, whilst I refrain from seeking out some obscure hiding place, where the countenance of man may never meet me more. It seems that Elise, actuated either by some inconceivable malice for our dismissing her, or bribed by my enemies, or making common cause with her infamous husband, has persuaded the Hoppners of a story so monstrous and incredible that they must have been prone to believe any evil to have believed such assertions upon such evidence. Mr. Hoppner wrote to Lord Byron to state this story as the reason why he declined any further communications with us, and why he advised him to do the same. Elise says that Claire was my mistress; that is very well, and so far there is nothing new; all the world has heard so much, and people may believe or not believe as they think good. She then proceeds to say that Claire was with child by me; that I gave her most violent medicine to procure abor-

275

tion; that this not succeeding she was brought to bed, and that I immediately tore the child from her and sent it to the Foundling Hospital—I quote Mr. Hoppner's words—and this is stated to have taken place in the winter after we left Este. In addition, she says that I treated *you* in the most shameful manner; that I neglected and beat you, and that Claire never let a day pass without offering you insults of the most violent kind, in which she was abetted by me.

"As to what Reviews and the world says, I do not care a jot, but when persons who have known me are capable of conceiving of me—not that I have fallen into a great error, as would have been the living with Claire as my mistress—but that I have committed such unutterable crimes as destroying or abandoning a child, and that my own! Imagine my despair of good!

"Imagine how it is possible that one of so weak and sensitive a nature can run further the gauntlet through this hellish society of men! *You* should write to the Hoppners, a letter refuting the charge, in case you believe, and know, and can prove that it is false, stating the grounds and proofs of your belief. I need not dictate what you should say, nor, I hope, inspire you with warmth to rebut a charge which you only can effectually rebut. If you will send the letter to me here, I will forward it to the Hoppners."

Mary Shelley to Shelley

"MY DEAR SHELLEY,

"Shocked beyond measure as I was, I instantly wrote the enclosed. If the task be not too dreadful, pray copy it for me. I cannot.

"Read that part of your letter which contains the accusation. I tried, but I could not write it. I think I could as soon have died. I send also Elise's last letter: enclose it or not as you think best.

"I wrote to you with far different feelings last night, beloved friend. Our barque is indeed 'tempest-tost' but love me, as you have ever done, and God preserve my child to me, and our enemies shall not be too much for us.

"Adieu, dearest! Take care of yourself—all yet is well. The shock for me is over, and I now despise the slander; but it must not pass uncontradicted. I sincerely thank Lord Byron for his kind unbelief.

"P.S. Do not think me imprudent in mentioning Claire's illness at Naples. It is well to meet facts. They are as cunning as wicked. I have read over my letter; it is written in haste,

277

but it were as well that the first burst of feeling should be expressed."

Mary Shelley to Mrs. Hoppner

"PISA, *Aug.* 10, 1821.

"After a silence of nearly two years, I address you again, and most bitterly do I regret the occasion on which I now write. . . .

"I write to defend him to whom I have the happiness to be united, whom I love and esteem beyond all living creatures, from the foulest calumnies; and to you I write this, who were so kind, and to Mr. Hoppner, to both of whom I indulged the pleasing idea that I have every reason to feel gratitude. This is indeed a painful task. Shelley is at present on a visit to Lord Byron at Ravenna, and I received a letter from him to-day, containing accounts that make my hand tremble so much that I can hardly hold the pen.

"He says Claire was Shelley's mistress, that . . . Upon my word, I solemnly assure you that I cannot write the words. I send you a part of Shelley's letter that you may see what I am now about to refute, but I had rather die than copy anything so vilely, so wickedly false, so beyond all imagination fiendish.

278

"But that you should believe it! That my beloved Shelley should stand thus slandered in your minds—he, the gentlest and most humane of creatures—is more painful to me than words can express. Need I say that the union between my husband and myself has ever been undisturbed? Love caused our first imprudence— love which, improved by esteem, a perfect trust one in the other, has increased daily and knows no bounds. . . .

"Those who know me well believe my simple word—it is not long ago that my father said in a letter to me that he had never known me utter a falsehood—but you, easy as you have been to credit evil, who may be more deaf to truth—to you I swear by all that I hold sacred upon heaven and earth, by a vow which I should die to write if I affirmed a falsehood—I swear by the life of my child, by my blessed beloved child, that I know the accusation to be false. But I have said enough to convince you, and are you not convinced? Repair, I conjure you, the evil you have done by retracting your confidence in one so vile as Elise, and by writing to me that you now reject as false every circumstance of her infamous tale.

"You were kind to us, and I will never forget it; now I require justice. You must believe me, and do me, I solemnly entreat you, the justice to confess that you do so."

Shelley showed this letter to Byron and asked for the address of Hoppner, but Byron begged to be allowed to send it himself.

"The Hoppners," he said, "had extracted a promise from me not to speak to you of this affair; in openly confessing that I have not kept my promise I must observe some form. That is why I wish to send the letter myself. My observations, besides, will give more weight to it."

Shelley readily consented and gave the letter to his host. Mary never received an answer.

.   .   .   .

The important question that Byron wished to discuss with Shelley was the fate of Allegra in case he—Byron—should leave Ravenna. Countess Guiccioli wished to go to Switzerland; Byron, who preferred Tuscany, begged Shelley to write to the Countess to describe life in Florence and Pisa in such attractive fashion that she would agree to go to one or the other.

Shelley had never seen his friend's mistress, but he was so used to be asked to intervene in the affairs of his acquaintance that he did not hesitate to write the letter asked, and it was so vigorous that it carried the day. It was suddenly decided that Byron and the Countess should join the Shelleys at Pisa. As to Allegra, Byron agreed to take her also. Claire not being there, he saw no reason for not doing so.

Before leaving Ravenna, Shelley went to see the child at the Convent of Bagna-Cavallo. He found her taller, but also more delicate and paler. Her lovely black hair fell in curls over her shoulders. She appeared in the midst of her companions as a being of a finer and nobler race. A kind of contemplative seriousness seemed to overlie her former vivacity.

She was shy at first, but Shelley, having given her a gold chain which he brought from Ravenna, she became more friendly. She led him to the convent garden, running and skipping so quickly that he could scarcely follow her; she showed him her little bed, her chair. He asked her what he should say to her mama.

"That she send me a kiss and a beautiful dress."
"And how do you wish the dress to be made?"
"And of silk and gold."

And to her father:

"That he come to see me and that he bring dear mother with him."

281

A difficult message to transmit to her noble father.

The dominant trait of the child seemed to Shelley to be vanity. Her education was defective, but she could recite a great many prayers by heart, spoke of Paradise, dreamed of it, and knew long lists of saints. This was the sort of training that Byron desired.

CHAPTER XXXII

MIRANDA

GREAT excitement such as travelling royalties always arouse reigned in the Pisan circle at the expected arrival of the Pilgrim. Mary, at Shelley's request, had taken for him the Palazzo Lanfranchi, stateliest on the Lung' Arno. Helped by the Williamses, she had done what she could to put this ancient palace in order. The vanguard arrived in the persons of the Guiccioli and her father, Count Gamba; the Shelleys gave them a cordial welcome. The Countess was an agreeable surprise. "She is a very pretty, sentimental, innocent Italian," Shelley wrote, "who, if I know anything of human nature and my Byron, will hereafter have plenty of opportunity to repent her rashness."

When Don Juan himself followed, all Pisa was at the windows to see the English Devil and his menagerie. The procession was well worth seeing; five carriages, six men-servants, nine horses, dogs, monkeys, peacocks, and ibises, all in line. The Shelleys were a little anxious as to what Byron would think of the palazzo, but fortunately it pleased him. He said he liked these old places dating back to the Middle Ages. In reality it dated to the sixteenth century, and was said to have been built from designs by Michael Angelo, but the noble lord always mixed up hopelessly architectural styles. The dark and damp cellars in particular delighted him. He spoke of them as dungeons and subterranean cells, and had cushions taken down so that he might sleep there.

He became at once the social centre of the Pisan circle, while Shelley remained its moral centre. Byron was visited from curiosity and admiration; Shelley from sympathy. Shelley got up early and read Goethe, Spinoza or Calderon until midday; then he was off to the pinewoods, where he worked in solitude until evening. Byron got up at midday and, after a light breakfast, went for a ride, or to practise pistol-shooting. In the evening he visited the Guiccioli, and coming home at eleven, would often work until two or three in the morning. Then in a state of feverish cerebral excitement, he would go to bed, sleep badly, and remain in bed half the following day.

The English in Pisa made a dead set at him.

Even the most Puritan amongst them could not
be severe on an authentic lord who brought to
them on foreign soil so delightful an epitome of
London's Vanity Fair. The pleasure he took in
giving scandal, what was it but a mark of orthodox respect? If indifference is justly considered
an offence, surely defiance must be accepted as a
token of humility? And was it not patent that
he could not exist without going into society,
paying court to women, accepting dinners and
returning them? He met with the greatest indulgence. But when he tried to win the same
for Shelley, the resistance was thoroughly British. In society Shelley was bored and did not
hide it. In questions of morality it was easy to
guess that he put the Spirit before the Letter,
that he believed in Redemption rather than in
Original Sin. Faith in the perfectibility of man
is naturally the most heinous of crimes, since, if
believed in, it would force one to work for man's
perfectibility. The mere smell of it makes society fly to arms for its destruction. All "nice"
women treated the Shelleys as pariahs and outcasts.

Shelley laughed at this, preferring a thousand
times the cool fresh air of night to the hot and
smoky atmosphere of card-rooms. But Mary
hankered to go everywhere. There was a cer-

tain Mrs. Beauclerc, gayest of English ladies in Pisa, who gave balls, "being afflicted," as Byron said, "with a litter of seven daughters all at the age when these animals are obliged to waltz for their livelihood." Mary's fixed idea was to be invited to one of these balls. "Everybody goes to them," she said. Shelley, distressed, looked up at the sky. "Everybody! Who is this mythical monster? Have you ever seen it, Mary?"

To win the favour of "everybody" she even went to Church Service, but the parson preached against Atheists, and kept looking at her in such a marked manner that, in spite of her desire to conform, her dignity as a wife prevented her from ever going again.

All these social worries, balls and dinner parties seemed to Shelley of an incredible vulgarity. When he was a boy of twenty, he had judged fashionable life as criminal, now it appeared to him contemptible, which was much more serious. To escape from Mary's absurd reproaches and regrets, he would take refuge with the Williamses. There he found anew the harmonious and affectionate atmosphere that was essential to him. Edward Williams had a gay, generous nature in which there was nothing petty. Jane's grace and sweetness, the gentleness of her movements, the soothing beauty of her voice, were as reposeful and pleasant as some delightful garden. Perhaps in his youth she would have pleased Shelley less. Then he dreamed always of heroic qualities in women, but to-day he asked from them the gift of forgetfulness rather than courage and strength.

Jane sang, and her voice carried him momentarily away from his tragic memories, and the chilly rectitude of his home. Just as formerly, when Harriet wounded him, and he read in Mary's eyes all the consolation they promised him, so now he contemplated in Jane's an image of the Antigone whom he had surely known and loved in a previous existence.

But he no longer considered it necessary to destroy in order to rebuild, to abandon Mary in order to fly with Jane. She was married to a good fellow, whose friend he wished loyally to remain, and it was necessary also to consider the feelings of Mary, poor unhappy woman. He was in love with Jane, but it was an immaterial love, without hope, and almost without desire.

She lent herself cleverly to the romantic business, would pass her hand through his hair, smooth his forehead, try to cure his sadness by her personal magnetism. She and her husband were as a marvellous fountain of friendship, at which a poet, weary of suffering, could cool his

287

fever. Jane and Edward were Ferdinand and
Miranda, the splendid, princely couple, and
Shelley was their faithful Ariel. . . . Round the
happy lovers flitted a captive, pure Spirit.

. . . .

The Williamses had often spoken to Shelley
of one of their friends, Trelawny, an extraordinary man, corsair and pirate, who at twenty-
eight had already led a life of adventure all the
world over, on land as well as on sea. He now
desired ardently to be admitted to the Pisa circle,
and he overwhelmed the Williamses with letters:
"If I come, shall I be able to know Shelley?
Above all, shall I be able to know Byron? Is
it possible to approach him?"

Williams, in daily intercourse with the two
Poets, no longer held them in any awe, so he replied with a touch of impatience, "Of course you
will see them. Shelley is the simplest of men.
. . . As to Byron, that will depend entirely on
yourself."

Trelawny reached Pisa late one evening and
went at once to the Tre Palazzi on the Lung'
Arno where the Williamses and the Shelleys
lived on different stories under the same roof.
He and the Williamses were in animated conversation when he perceived in the passage near the
open door a pair of glittering eyes steadily fixed
288

on his. Jane, going to the doorway, laughingly said, "Come in, Shelley, it's only our friend Tre just arrived."

Shelley glided in, blushing like a girl, and holding out his two hands gave the sailor's a warm pressure. Trelawny looked at him with surprise. It was hard to believe that this flushed and artless face could be that of the genius and rebel, reviled as a monster in England, and whom the Lord Chancellor had deprived of his rights as a father. Shelley, on his side, admired Trelawny's bold, wild face, raven-black moustache, handsome half-Arab type. Both of them were so astounded they could find nothing to say. To relieve their embarrassment, Jane asked Shelley what book he had in his hand.

His face brightened and he answered briskly: "Calderon's *Magico Prodigioso*. I am translating some passages in it."

"Oh, read it to us!"

Immediately Shelley, shoved off from the shore of commonplace incidents that could not interest him, began to translate from the open book, in so masterly a manner, with such perfection of form, that Trelawny no longer doubted his identity.

A dead silence followed the reading. Trelawny looked up and seeing no one asked, "Where is he?"

"Who?" said Jane. "Shelley? Oh, he comes and goes like a spirit no one knows when or where."

The next day it was Shelley himself who took Trelawny to call on Byron. Here the surroundings were very different. A large marble hall, a giant staircase, powdered footmen and surly dogs. Trelawny, like every one else, saw in Byron's external appearance all the traits with which imagination endows genius, but the great man's conversation struck him as commonplace. He seemed, too, to be playing a part, and an out-of-date one—that of a rake-hell of the Regency. He told stories about actors, boxers and hard-drinkers, and of how he had swum the Hellespont. Of this exploit he was very proud.

At three the horses were brought round. After riding for a couple of hours, the party dismounted at a small *podere,* pistols were sent for, a cane was stuck into the ground behind the house and a piece of money placed in a slit at the top of the cane. Byron, Shelley and Trelawny fired at fifteen paces, and their firing was pretty equal. Each time the cane or the coin was hit by one or the other. Trelawny was pleased to see that despite his feminine appearance Shelley could hold his own with men.

On the way back they talked poetry, and Trelawny cited a couplet from *Don Juan* as an example of felicitous rhyming. Byron, won over, brought his horse round to trot beside him.

"Confess now," said he, "you expected to find me a Timon of Athens or a Timur the Tartar, and you're surprised to find a man of the world —never in earnest—laughing at all things mundane?"

Then he muttered as to himself:

> The world is a bundle of hay;
> Mankind are the asses who pull.

．　　．　　．　　．　　．　　．　　．

Trelawny returned with Shelley and Mary. "How different Byron is to anything one expects of him!" said he. "There's no mystery about him at all. On the contrary he talks too freely, and says things he had much better not say. He seems as jealous and impulsive as a woman, and maybe is more dangerous."

"Mary," said Shelley, "Trelawny has found out Byron already. How stupid we were—how long it took us."

"The reason is," said Mary, "that Trelawny lives with the living, and we live with the dead."

CHAPTER XXXIII

THE DISCIPLES

THE sailor who had come to Pisa to admire two great men found that it was he, on the contrary, who was admired by them. It is true that when Trelawny was absent, Byron said of him: "If we could get him to wash his hands and not to tell lies, we might make a gentleman of him," but when he was present Byron treated him with the greatest respect. Like all artists Byron and Shelley wrote in order to console themselves for not living, and a man of action appeared to these two men of dreams as a strange and enviable phenomenon.

Shelley consulted Trelawny as to nautical terms, and drew with him, on the sandy shores of the Arno, keels, sails, and sea-charts. "I've missed my vocation," said he. "I ought to have been a sailor."

"A man who neither smokes nor swears can never be a sailor," Trelawny told him.

Byron, an imaginary corsair, would have liked

to learn from a real corsair the ways and customs of the brotherhood, and did his utmost in Trelawny's company to talk in cynical and bravado fashion. Trelawny, quick to perceive his influence over Byron, tried to make use of it in the service of Shelley.

"You know," said he as they rode together one day, "that you might help Shelley a good deal at small cost by a friendly word or two in your next work, such as you have given to other writers of much less merit."

"All trades have their secrets," Byron answered. "If we crack up a popular author, he repays us in the same coin, capital and interest. But Shelley! A bad investment. . . . Who reads the Snake? . . . Besides, if he cast off the slough of his mystifying metaphysics, he would want no puffing."

"But why do your London friends treat him so cavalierly? They rarely notice him when they meet him at your place. Yet he is as wellborn and bred as any of them. What are they afraid of?"

Byron smiled and whispered in Trelawny's ear:

"Shelley is not a Christian."

"Are they?"

"Ask them."

"If I met the Devil at your table," said Tre-lawny, "I should treat him as a friend of yours."

The Pilgrim looked at him keenly to see if there were a double meaning, then moving his horse up nearer said in a low voice of admirably acted fear and respect:

"The Devil is a Royal Personage."

.   .   .   .

With the Williamses, Trelawny was more outspoken. The three of them formed the chorus to the tragedy; knowing they were not made for the chief parts, they took pleasure in commenting upon the acting of those who were.

"One might imagine," said Trelawny, "that Byron is jealous of Shelley. Yet Murray is obliged to call on the police to protect his premises every time he publishes a new canto of *Childe Harold,* while poor Shelley hasn't got ten readers. Byron has high birth, riches, beauty, glory, love . . ."

"Yes," Williams interrupted, "but Byron is the slave to his passions and to any woman who is at all decided. Shelley in his nutshell of a boat floats in mid-stream on the Arno, and refuses to let it carry him away. His ideas are well-grounded, he holds a doctrine. Byron is incapable of holding one for two consecutive hours. He is well aware of this, and can't forgive

294

himself for it. You see it in the triumphant tone in which he speaks of Shelley's misfortunes."

"Byron," said Jane, "is a spoiled child, but neither he nor Shelley understands men. Shelley loves them too much, and Byron not enough."

"What's so terrible about Shelley," said Trelawny, "is that he has not the smallest instinct of self-preservation. . . . The other day when I was diving in the Arno, he said he so much regretted not being able to swim. 'Try,' said I. 'Put yourself on your back, and you'll float to begin with.'

"He stripped and jumped in without the smallest hesitation. He sank to the bottom and lay there like a conger-eel, not making the least movement to save himself. He would have drowned if I had not instantly fished him out."

Jane sighed, knowing how much the thought of suicide haunted Shelley's mind. He often repeated that nearly every one he had loved had died in this way.

"Yet he doesn't seem unhappy?"

"No, because he lives in his dreams. But in real life don't you think he suffers from the impossibility of spreading his ideas, from his books that don't sell, from his unhappy home life? Death must often appear to him like the awakening from a nightmare."

"He believes in a future life," said Trelawny.
"Those who call him an Atheist don't know him.
He has often told me that he thinks the French
philosophy of the eighteenth century false and
pernicious. Plato and Dante have overcome
Diderot for him. All the same he doesn't regret
his attitude towards established religion. . . .
'Why,' I asked him, 'do you call yourself an
Atheist? It annihilates your chances in this
world.' 'It is a word of abuse,' said he, 'to stop
discussion, a painted Devil to frighten fools. I
used it to express my abhorrence of superstition.
I took it up as a knight takes up a gauntlet, in
defiance of injustice. The delusions of Chris-
tianity are fatal to genius and originality; they
limit thought.' "

Thus spoke the chorus in unanimity, and did
not perhaps perceive that their adoration of
Shelley fed and grew on his misfortunes. We
are more inclined to love that which we can pity
than that which we must admire. Man finds in
the spectacle of unmerited failure flattering arguments which explain his own ill-luck. The
blend of admiration and compassion is one of the
surest recipes for love. It would have needed
much humility of mind for Williams and Trelawny to have the same affection for the brilliant Byron that they had for poor dear Shelley

THE DISCIPLES

While the disciples discoursed in this fashion, the Master worked in the pine-woods outside Pisa. There the sea-winds had thrown down one of the pines, which now hung suspended over a deep pool of glimmering water. Under the lea of the trunk, and nearly hidden, sat the Poet like some wild thing, the way to his retreat pointed out by quantities of scattered papers, covered with the scrawls of unfinished poems.

When in his day-dreaming he forgot everything, even the dinner hour, Mary and Trelawny would go off to find him. Tre had constituted himself *cavalier' sirvente* to the forsaken lady, and paid her court in corsair-fashion which she, in her honest woman-way, found very amusing.

The loose sand and hot sun soon knocked her up. She sat down under the cool canopy of the pines and Trelawny continued the Poet-chase alone. He found him at last, but so absorbed by some inner vision, that to avoid startling him, Trelawny drew his attention first by the crackling of the pine-needles. He picked up an Æschylus, a Shakespeare, then a scribbled paper: "To Jane with a guitar": but he could only make out the two first lines:

> Ariel to Miranda. Take
> This slave of music. . . .

He hailed him, and Shelley, turning his head, answered faintly, "Hello! Come in."

"Is this your study?" Trelawny asked.

"Yes," he answered, "and these trees are my books—they tell no lies. In composing, one's faculties must not be divided: in a house there is no solitude: a door shutting, a footstep heard, a bell ringing, a voice, causes an echo in your brain, and dissolves your visions."

"Here you have the river rushing by you, the birds chattering . . ."

"The river flows by like Time, and all the sounds of Nature harmonize. . . . It is only the human animal that is discordant and disturbs me. Oh, how difficult it is to know why we are here, a perpetual torment to ourselves and to every living thing!"

Trelawny interrupted to tell him that his wife was waiting for him at the edge of the wood. He started up, snatched up his scattered books and papers and thrust them into his hat and jacket pockets, sighing, "Poor Mary! hers is a sad fate. She can't bear solitude, nor I society—the quick coupled with the dead."

He began to proffer excuses to her, but she, either to hide her emotions or from a Godwinesque lack of any, began in a bantering tone: "What a wild goose you are, Percy! If my thoughts have strayed from my book, it was to the Opera, and my new dress from Florence, and especially to the ivy wreath so much admired for my hair, and not to you, you silly fellow! When I left home my satin slippers had not arrived. These are serious matters. . . ."

But in Mary's pleasantries there was always a note which rang false.

CHAPTER XXXIV

II SAMUEL XII: 23

BYRON, after promising Shelley to bring Allegra to Pisa, arrived without her, and Claire, who had come expressly from Florence to wait about the city in the hopes of seeing the child, was horribly alarmed on learning she had been left in the convent of Bagno-Cavallo. Her Italian friends gave her a sinister description of this convent, set down in the middle of the marshes of the Romagna, and in the most unhealthy climate. The nuns—Capucins—ignored hygiene, fed the children disgracefully, and did not warm them at all. Claire could not see a fire without thinking of her poor little darling who never saw or felt a cheerful blaze.

This high-spirited young woman was brought, through maternal anguish, to an abnegation that was sublime. She wrote to Byron that she would renounce ever seeing Allegra again so long as she lived, if he would consent to put her in a good English school. "I can no longer resist," she said, "the internal inexplicable feeling which haunts me that I shall never see her any more."

Byron made no reply. There was some talk amongst Claire's friends of rescuing Allegra by stratagem, but Shelley begged her to have patience. While agreeing with her as to Byron's cruelty, he disapproved of thoughtless violence. . . . "Lord Byron is inflexible and you are in his power. Remember, Claire, when you rejected my earnest advice, and checked me with that contempt which I had never merited from you at Milan and how vain is now your regret! This is the second of my sibylline volumes. If you wait for the third, it may be sold at a still higher price."

He called upon Byron to plead Claire's cause, but the moment Byron heard her name he gave an impatient shrug of the shoulders. "Oh, women can't exist without making scenes!" Shelley told him what Claire had heard about the unsuitability of the convent. "What do I know about it?" said he. "I have never been there." Then, when Claire's anguish and her fears were described to him, a smile of malicious satisfaction passed over his face.

"I had difficulty in restraining myself from knocking him down," said Shelley afterwards at

Lady Mountcashell's. "I was furious but I was wrong. He can no more help being what he is than that door can help being a door."

But old Mr. Tighe told him, "You are quite wrong in your fatalism. If I were to horsewhip that door it would still remain a door, but if Lord Byron were well horsewhipped my opinion is he would become as humane as he is now inhuman. It's the subserviency of his friends that makes him the insolent tyrant he is."

On hearing of Shelley's failure, Claire fell into such despair that Mary and Shelley would not allow her to return to Florence alone amongst strangers. They were going to spend the summer at the sea with the Williamses and they invited her to go with them.

Shelley looked forward with eagerness to this plan. Williams and he had consulted Trelawny about a boat, and he was having one built for them at Genoa by Captain Roberts, a friend of his. They had already christened her the *Don Juan* in honour of Byron, who had also commissioned Roberts to build him a schooner with a covered-in deck: the *Bolivar*.

Shelley and Williams saw themselves masters of the Mediterranean. Their wives were less enthusiastic. While the two young men drew charts of the bay upon the sand, Mary and Jane walked together, philosophized, and picked violets by the roadside.

"I hate this boat!" said Mary.

"So do I," Jane agreed. "But it's no use saying anything, it would do no good and merely spoil their pleasure."

So as to put their projects into action, two houses were necessary at the seaside. They thought of the Bay of Spezzia. Shelley and Williams hunted for these houses along its shores in vain. Lord Byron, who wished to join them, must have a palazzo, but he was obliged to give up the idea at once, since even two fisherman's houses were not to be had. Williams and his wife determined to make one last search; to distract Claire from her troubles they took her with them.

They had left Pisa but a few hours when Lord Byron wrote to Shelley that he had received bad news of Allegra. An epidemic of typhus had broken out in the Romagna. The nuns had taken no preventative measures. The child, already weak and tired, had caught the fever. She was dead. "I do not know," he added, "that I have anything to reproach in my conduct and certainly nothing in my feelings and intentions towards the dead. But it is a moment when we are apt to think that, if this or that had been done such events might have been prevented—though every day and hour shows us that they are the most natural and inevitable. I suppose that Time will do his usual work—Death has done his."

The Shelleys went to call on him. He was paler than usual, but as calm as ever.

Two days later the Williamses and Claire came back from their expedition. Shelley, fearing some act of violence on her part, if she were told of her misfortune while in Byron's neighbourhood, resolved to say nothing to her so long as they remained in Pisa.

Williams had not found the two furnished houses he sought. Along the entire coast there was but one house to let, a big unfurnished and abandoned building known as the Casa Magni at Lerici, with a veranda facing the sea and almost over it.

Shelley, who desired above all things to get Claire out of Pisa, decided to take the Casa Magni. The two households must live together. Inconvenient? That didn't matter. No furniture? Furniture could be sent from Pisa. When Shelley was really determined on a thing, nothing could resist him. "I go forward," said he, "until I am stopped. But nothing ever does stop me."

The Custom House officials, the boatmen, raised scores of difficulties. Shelley brushed them aside by the sheer force of a will-power that takes no notice of the outside world, and in a few days the two families were settled in at the seaside.

    .   .   .   .

Casa Magni had been a Jesuit convent. It was a white house standing almost in the sea, and backing against a forest. A terrace, supported on arches, overhung the superb Bay of Spezzia. The ground floor was unpaved and uninhabitable, being reached by the waves when the sea was rough. It was used simply for storing boat-gear and fishing-tackle. The single story over this was divided into a large hall or saloon, and four small bedrooms which opened from it: two for Shelley and Mary, one for the Williamses and one for Claire. The accommodation was scanty, and the first evening depressing. Down below the waves beat against the rocks with a mournful persistency. The Williamses and Shelleys could think of nothing but Claire, and she, with no idea of the dreadful truth, imagined they were annoyed at having her there with them in a house which was obviously too small. She said so, and offered to go back to Florence. Every one cried out against this. Jane whispered something to Mary, and the two withdrew to the Williamses' room. Shelley joined them. Claire went towards the room after a moment or two: she found them in eager conversation which instantly ceased as they saw her. Then before a single word had been uttered, she said:

"Allegra is dead?"

The next day she wrote Byron a terrible letter, which he returned to Shelley, complaining of Claire's harshness towards him, and begging Shelley to let her know he would allow her to make any arrangements she liked for the burial of their child.

She replied with a sombre irony that for the future she left everything to him, and that all she asked was a portrait of Allegra and a piece of her hair. Byron become surprisingly pliable, sent almost at once a very pretty miniature and a dark curl.

Claire took leave of her friends at Casa Magni, and went back to Florence to live amongst strangers, who, knowing nothing of her grief, could do nothing to revive it.

Byron decided to have his daughter buried in

England, in the church of Harrow-on-the-Hill,
where he had been at school, and to place on the
wall above the grave a marble tablet with the
words:

> To the Memory of Allegra
> Daughter of George Gordon Lord Byron
> Died at Bagna-Cavallo, the 20th April, 1822.
> Aged five years and six months.
>
> I shall go to her, but she shall
> not return to me.
>
> II Sam. xii: 23.

But the Rector of Harrow and the church-
wardens considered it immoral to admit into their
church the body of an illegitimate child, more
particularly if the epitaph disclosed the name of
the father. Allega was therefore buried outside
the church, and with no inscription, which was of
course the proper thing to do.

Lord Byron, who had never set foot inside the
convent of Bagna-Cavallo while Allegra was
alive, went to visit it some time after the child's
death, for now his regrets lent it a romantic and
sentimental interest. It inspired him with a
fine meditation on death and on himself: "I shall
go to her, but she shall not return to me."

The second Samuel was quite right.

CHAPTER XXXV

THE REFUGE

SHELLEY was charmed with Casa Magni. He liked the wild solitude of the place, the forest behind the house, the rocky and wooded bays and the fishermen's poor villages.

But Mary felt lost and unhappy. Again pregnant, anxious, irritable, she would have much preferred to live in a city near a good doctor. She thought the peasantry uncouth and hateful, their *Genovese* jargon disgusted her as much as the dialect of Tuscany had pleased her. The presence of Jane Williams, so appreciated by her at Pisa, began to get on her nerves. Housekeeping in common is for women the acid test. There were stupid quarrels over servants and frying-pans. Shelley spoke too warmly of Jane's perfection, and wrote her too divine serenades.

To all Mary's grumblings he replied with his usual sweetness. With the utmost tenderness he caressed and consoled her. "Poor Mary," he said of her, "it is the curse of Tantalus to be en-

308

dowed with such fine qualities, and yet unable
to excite the sympathy indispensable to their application to domestic life."

He knew he could not change her, that her
physical condition explained a good deal of her
peevishness, which he bore with patient affection.
What she constantly reproached him with was
his complete indifference to the things that other
men thought worth while. She still admired him
as much as ever, in him alone she found the
strength on which to lean. But why could he
never use this strength to his own advantage? He
seemed to have no notion of his own interests.
His personality was not in his own eyes what
theirs is for men in general, something strictly
limited by definite boundaries; no, his poured out-
wards in a sort of luminous fringe melting into
that of his friends, and even into that of perfect
strangers. As to the customs and cares of human
societies, he continued to ignore them.

Every month he went to Leghorn to draw his
allowance. He brought back a bagful of *scudi*
which he emptied out upon the floor. Then with
the fire-shovel he gathered the coins together in
a heap, which he flattened out into a sort of cake
with his foot. Always with the shovel he cut
the cake into two parts. One was for Mary
rent and housekeeping. The other half was again

309

divided into two, of which one went to **Mary as** pin-money, and the other remained for **Percy.** But Mary knew what was meant by "for Percy": it was for Godwin despite all vows, for Claire, for the Hunts . . .

One day Captain Roberts was expected over to luncheon from Genoa. Conscious that their anchorite way of living would not suit ordinary mortals, there was considerable commotion at the villa, but notwithstanding the bother and turmoil the three women, as is woman's wont, seemed to enjoy it. The visitor came and he was most anxious to see the Poet of whom he had heard so much, but Shelley had disappeared. They sat down to table without him. Suddenly one of the trio of ladies cried out, "Oh my gracious!" and Mary, turning round, saw Shelley completely naked crossing the room, and trying to hide behind the maidservant.

"Percy, how dare you!" she cried, which was imprudent, for Shelley, considering himself unjustly attacked, abandoned his refuge and came up to the table to explain. The ladies covered their faces with their hands. Yet he was good to look at, his hair full of seaweed, his slender body wet and scented with the salt of the sea.

But the daughter of William Godwin had **a** horror of such unconventional happenings.

310

THE REFUGE

Shelley and Williams waited for their boat with the impatience of schoolboys, and the moment a strange sail, coming from the direction of Leghorn, doubled the point of Lerici, they rushed down to the beach.

After Allegra's death Shelley had written to Roberts to change the name of his boat from the *Don Juan* to the *Ariel*. Everything which reminded him of Byron was now hateful to him. Great therefore was his surprise and anger, when on the arrival of his little yacht, he saw painted in enormous letters in the middle of the mainsail: *Don Juan*. Byron, told of the change of name, had forced Roberts, in spite of Shelley's orders, to print the sign of the Devil upon the Platonic bark. Armed with hot water, soap and brushes, Shelley and Williams set to work to wash out the infamy from their poor boat. They had no success. They tried turpentine, which failed equally. Then they consulted specialists, who were of opinion that a bit of sail would have to be cut clean out and a new piece inserted; nothing short of this could mend the case. Shelley had the operation performed at once.

The Genoese captain who had sailed the boat to Lerici said that she sailed and worked well, but was a ticklish boat to manage. Shelley and Williams, enthusiastic but incompetent yachts·

men, had insisted on having her built to a design
made by a naval officer for Williams, before he
left England. The lovely sweeping lines of the
model enchanted them, but the boat when built
to plan required a couple of tons of iron ballast
to bring her down to her bearings, and even then
was very cranky in a breeze.

The two owners of the *Ariel* determined to
man her themselves, with the help of Charles
Vivian, a young sailor. Shelley was awkward
as a woman in all things appertaining to boats,
but full of good intentions. He tangled himself
up in the rigging, read Sophocles while trying
to steer, and several times just missed falling
overboard. But never in his life had he been so
happy. When Trelawny saw his seamanship, he
took Williams by the arm and advised him to add
to the crew a Genoese accustomed to the coast.
Williams was hurt . . . three seasoned sailors
such as they . . . and was he not Captain? And
had he not Shelley?

"Shelley! You'll never do any good with him
until you shear the wisps of hair that hang over
his eyes, heave his Greek Poets overboard, and
plunge his arms up to the elbow in a tar-bucket."

The *Ariel* drew too much water to be run on
shore at Casa Magni, so Williams with the aid
of a carpenter built a tiny dinghy of basket-

work, covered with tarred canvas. It was a fragile toy which upset at a touch. The Poet was delighted with it, although it capsized continually, and gave him many a ducking.

One evening, as he dragged the skiff out from the house, he saw Jane and her two children on the sands. He invited her to bring them for a row. "With careful stowage," said he, "there is room for us all in my barge." She squatted in the bottom of the frail skiff with her babies, and the gunwale sank to within six inches of the water; a puff of wind, the smallest movement of any one of them, and it must cant over, fill, and glide from under them.

Jane understood that Percy intended to float on the water near the shore, but he, proud to show a lovely woman how well he sculled, bent to his oars, and they were soon out on the blue waters of the bay. Then, shipping the oars, he fell into a deep reverie. Jane was seized with the most awful terror. There was no eye watching them, no boat within a mile, the shore fast receding, the water deepening, and the Poet dreaming. She made several remarks, but they met with no response.

Suddenly he raised his head, his face brightened as with a bright thought, and he exclaimed,

313

joyfully, "Now let us together solve the great mystery!"

Had Jane uttered a cry, her children were lost. Shelley might make a sudden movement, the bark would capsize, the waters wrap them round as a winding-sheet. . . . Suppressing her terror, she answered promptly. "No, thank you, not now. I should like my dinner first and so would the children . . . And look, there is Edward coming on shore with Trelawny . . . they'll be so surprised at our being out at this time, and Edward says this boat is not safe."

"Safe!" cried the Poet, "I'd go to Leghorn or anywhere in her."

Jane felt that the Angel of Death, who always attended the Poet on the water, now spread his wings and vanished.

"You haven't yet written the words for the Indian air," she said carelessly.

"Yes, I have," he answered, "but you must play me the air again, and I'll try and make the thing better."

Meanwhile he had paddled his cockleshell into shallow water; as soon as Jane saw the sandy bottom, she snatched up her babies, and clambered out so hurriedly that the punt was turned over and the Poet pinned down underneath it.

He rose with it on his back, like a hermit-crab in any old empty shell.

"Jane, are you mad?" cried her husband, surprised at her lubberly way of getting out of a boat. "Had you waited a moment, we would have hauled the boat up."

"No, thank you. Oh, I have escaped the most dreadful fate! Never will I put my foot in that horrid coffin again. 'Solve the great mystery'! . . . Why, he is the greatest of all mysteries! Who can predict what he will do? . . . He is seeking after what we all avoid—death. I wish we were away. I shall always be in terror."

But the Poet's boyish face wore its accustomed innocent and radiant expression. During this glorious summer, nothing seemed able to mar his joy. Of an evening he liked to go sailing in the *Ariel* by moonlight. Mary sitting at his feet, her head against his knees, remembered how she had sat thus on the stormy cross-channel journey ten years ago. Ten years . . . what quantities of things had happened in ten years. How much subtler, crueller, and more treacherous Life had been, than either of them had then imagined.

Sitting in the stern, Jane sang an Indian serenade, accompanying it on the guitar, while Shelley gazed up into the dark blue sky of June, where the moon burned inextinguishably beautiful, suffusing the mountain-clouds with intolerable brilliancy. His mind was emptied of thought, his senses annihilated in a delicious ecstasy; his soul, clipt in a net woven of dew-beams, seemed to be floating on waves of love and odour and deep melody. He walked again among the splendid visions, the crystalline palaces, the iridescent vapours, which during so long a time had appeared to him the sole reality. He knew today that there existed another universe, a harsh and inflexible one, but in these high regions, only animated by the liquid and undulating sweetness of song, by the invisible movement of luminous spheres, in these regions the jealousy of women, money worries, political quarrels, appeared so infinitely petty that they could not touch his wild, sweet, incommunicable happiness. He would have liked to swoon away in ravishment while saying with Faust to the passing moment, "Verweile doch! Du bist so schön."

CHAPTER XXXVI

ARIEL SET FREE

FOR a long time, Shelley had wished to bring out to Italy his friends, the Hunts, to whom their creditors and political enemies gave a hard life in England. He offered to pay the journey, but he would not be able, naturally, to support them and their seven children. He had talked so much about this to Byron that he had obtained from him a promise to found with Hunt a liberal newspaper to be published in Italy, and which would enjoy copyright of all Byron's works, a privilege sufficient in itself to assure the success of the newspaper, and to make Hunt's fortune. It was a very generous offer on Byron's part, who had nothing to gain by the association with Hunt, but a good deal to lose. He did more, however; he would allow the Hunts to occupy the ground floor of the Palazzo Lanfranchi, which Shelley on his side undertook to furnish. Everything being thus settled, the whole Hunt tribe set out.

After incredible difficulties and delays they arrived at Leghorn by the end of June, 1822. Trelawny on the *Bolivar* was waiting for them in the harbour. Shelley and Williams arrived on the *Ariel,* scudding into port in fine style. Shelley was inexpressibly delighted to see Hunt, and set off with him and the tribe for Pisa. Williams remained at Leghorn to await the return of his friend, when they would sail home together.

Unfortunately Hunt's immediate contact with Byron was far from pleasant. Although Byron considered Hunt's political ideas extreme, nevertheless he had a sort of protective affection for him, considering him an honest writer, a good father and husband, a decent sort of fellow. But he had never been able to endure Hunt's wife, whom he considered a dowdy and disagreeable woman as impertinent as she was silly. Marianne Hunt was a type of the equalitarian who can never for a moment forget inequalities. To show that she was not impressed by Byron's wealth and position, she treated him with an insolence that a chimney-sweep would not have tolerated. With the kind-hearted and charming Countess Guiccioli she put on the airs and graces of an outraged British matron.

Byron remained courteous, but became glacial. At the end of twenty-four hours he could endure no more. Seven disorderly children romped up and down the Palazzo, spoiling everything. "A Kraal of Hottentots, dirtier and more mischievous than Yahoos." He looked with disgust on such human vermin, and put his big bulldog to guard the staircase: "Don't let any little cockneys pass our way!" he told him and patted his head.

Already he was sick of the newspaper.

Shelley, who should have left the same day, could not forsake Hunt without having settled the business. He got round Byron, lectured Marianne, consoled poor Hunt, and delayed his departure from day to day until everything was arranged. His tenacity always triumphed over Byron's haughty lassitude.

He obtained the promise that the first number of the new paper should have the copyright of *The Vision of Judgment*, which Byron had recently finished. This would give Hunt a first-rate send-off.

Williams, waiting at Leghorn, grew impatient and testy. Never before, he complained, had he been separated from his wife for so many days. Shelley sent him letter after letter to explain the delay.

The July heat was suffocating; *"le soleil d'Italie au rire impitoyable."* The peasants stopped working in the fields from ten to five. There was a water shortage, and processions of priests carried round miraculous statues and prayed for rain.

On the morning of the 8th, Trelawny and Shelley arrived from Pisa. They went to Shelley's bank, made purchases for the housekeeping at Casa Magni, and then the two friends and Williams went down to the harbour. Trelawny wanted to accompany the *Ariel* on the *Bolivar*. The sky was clouding over, and a light wind blowing in the direction of Lerici. Captain Roberts predicted a storm. Williams, who was in a hurry to be off, declared that in seven hours they would be at home.

At midday Shelley, Williams, and Charles Vivian were on board the *Ariel*. Trelawny on the *Bolivar* was getting ready too. The guard-boat boarded them to overhaul their papers: "La barchetta *Don Juan?* Il capitano Percy Shelley? Va bene."

Trelawny, who had not got his port-clearance, tried to brazen it out. The officer of the Health Office threatened him with fourteen days' quarantine. He proposed to go instantly and obtain the clearance papers, but Williams, fretting and fuming, would not hear another word. There was no more time to be lost. It was two o'clock already, and there was so little wind they would have great difficulty in reaching home before night.

Between two and three o'clock the *Ariel* sailed out of harbour almost at the same moment with two feluccas. Trelawny re-anchored sullenly, furled his sails, and with a ship's glass watched the progress of his friends. His Genovese mate said to him, "They should have sailed this morning at three or four a.m. instead of three p.m. She is standing too much in shore; the current will fix her there."

Trelawny replied, "She will soon have the land-breeze."

"Maybe she will soon have too much breeze," remarked the mate. "That gaff top-sail is foolish in a boat with no deck and no sailor on board . . . Look at those black lines and the dirty rags hanging on them out of the sky, look at the smoke on the water! The Devil is brewing mischief."

Standing on the end of the mole Captain Roberts also kept the boat in view. When he could see her no longer, he got leave to ascend the lighthouse-tower whence he could again discern her about ten miles out at sea. A storm was visibly coming from the Gulf, and he perceived

321

that the *Ariel* was taking in her top-sail. Then
the haze of the storm hid her completely.

In the harbour it was oppressively sultry.
The heaviness of the atmosphere and an un-
wonted stillness benumbed the senses. Trelawny went to his cabin and fell asleep in spite
of himself. He was aroused by noises overhead:
the men were getting up a chain cable to let go
another anchor. There was a general stir
amongst the shipping, getting-down yards and
masts, veering out cables, letting-go anchors. It
was very dark. The sea looked as solid and
smooth as a sheet of lead and was covered with
an oily scum: gusts of wind swept over it without ruffling it, and big drops of rain fell on its
surface rebounding as if they could not penetrate
it. Fishing-craft under bare poles rushed by in
shoals running foul of the ships in the harbour.
But the din and hubbub made by men and their
shrill pipings were suddenly silenced by the
crashing voice of a thunder-squall that burst
right overhead.

When, twenty minutes later, the horizon was
in some degree cleared, Trelawny and Roberts
looked anxiously seaward in the hopes of descry-
ing Shelley's boat amongst the many small craft
scattered about. No trace of her was to be seen.

On the other side of the bay two women waited for news. Mary was uneasy and depressed. The excessive heat of the summer frightened her. It was during such a summer that little Willie had died, and she looked at the baby in her arms with terror. He seemed certainly in the best of health; nevertheless, standing on the terrace gazing on one of the most lovely views in the world, she was oppressed with wretchedness. Her eyes kept filling with tears, she knew not why. "Yet," thought she, "when he, when my Shelley returns, I shall be happy— he will comfort me; if my boy be ill, he will restore him and encourage me."

On the Monday, Jane had a letter from her husband dated Saturday. He said that Shelley was still detained at Pisa, "but if he should not come by Monday, I will come in a felucca, and you may expect me on Thursday evening at furthest." This Monday was the fatal Monday, the day of the storm.

But Mary and Jane never imagined for a moment that the *Ariel* could have put to sea in such weather. On Tuesday it rained all day, and the sea was calm. On Wednesday the wind was fair from Leghorn, and several feluccas arrived thence. The skipper of one of these said that the *Ariel* had sailed on the Monday, but

neither Jane nor Mary believed him. Thursday
was another day of fair wind, and the two
women kept continuous watch from the terrace.
Every instant they hoped to see the tall sails
of the little boat double the promontory. At
midnight they were still watching and still without any sight of the boat, and they began to
fear—not the truth—but that some illness, some
disagreeable occurrence, had detained their husbands in Leghorn. As the hours went on, Jane
became so miserable that she determined to hire
a boat next day and go to Leghorn herself. But
next day brought with it a heavy sea and a contrary wind. No boatman would venture out.

At midday came letters. There was one from
Hunt for Shelley. Mary opened it trembling
all over. Hunt said: "Pray write to tell us how
you got home, for they say that you had bad
weather after you sailed on Monday, and we are
anxious."

The letter fell from her hands. Jane picked
it up, read it, and said, "Then it is all over!"

"No, my dear Jane, it is not all over, but this
suspense is dreadful! Come with me—we will
go to Leghorn. We will post to be swift and
learn our fate."

The road from Lerici to Leghorn passes by
Pisa. They stopped at Lord Byron's house to

see if there was any news. They knocked at the door, and some one called out "Chi é?" for it was already late in the evening. It was the Guicciolis' maid. Lord Byron was in bed, but the Countess, all smiles, came down to meet them. On seeing the terrifying aspect of Mary's face, very white, looking like marble, she stopped astonished.

"Where is he? Sapete alcuna cosa di Shelley?" said Mary. Byron, who followed his *dama*, knew nothing more than that Shelley had left Pisa the preceding Sunday, and had sailed on Monday in bad weather.

It was now midnight, but refusing to rest the two women went on to Leghorn, which they reached at two o'clock in the morning. Their coachman took them to the wrong inn, where they found neither Trelawny nor Captain Roberts. They threw themselves dressed on their beds and waited for daylight. At six o'clock they visited all the inns of the town one after the other, and at the *Globe* Roberts came down to them with a face which told them that the worst was true. They learned from him all that had occurred during that agonizing week.

Yet hope was not entirely extinct. The *Ariel* might have been blown to Corsica, or Elba, or even farther. They sent a courier from tower

325

to tower along the coast as far as Nice to know if anything had been seen or found, and at 9 a.m. they quitted Leghorn for Casa Magni. Trelawny went with them. At Via Reggio they were told that a punt, a water-keg, and some bottles had been cast upon the beach. Trelawny went to look at them, and recognized the little skiff of the *Ariel.* But there was the possibility that, finding it cumbersome in bad weather, they had thrown it overboard.

When Jane and Mary reached home, the village was holding high festival. The noise of dancing, laughing and singing kept them awake the whole night through.

. . . .

Five or six days later Trelawny, who had promised a reward to any of the coastguard who should send him news, was called to Via Reggio, where a body had been washed up by the sea. It was a corpse terrible to look upon, for the face and hands and those parts of the body not protected by the clothes had been eaten away by the fish. But the tall slight figure, the jacket, the volume of Sophocles in one pocket, and Keats's poems in the other, doubled back as if the reader, in the act of reading, had hastily thrust it away, were all too familiar to Trelawny to leave a doubt on his mind that this mutilated body was any

326

other than Shelley's. Almost at the same time the corpse of Williams was found not far off, more mutilated still, and three weeks later a third body was found, that of Charles Vivian, the sailor boy, about four miles from the other two. It was a mere skeleton.

Trelawny had the remains buried temporarily in the sand to preserve them from the sea, and galloped off towards Casa Magni.

At the threshold of the house he stopped. There was no one to be seen . . . a lamp burned in the big room . . . perhaps the two widows were suggesting to one another new grounds for hope. . . . Trelawny thought of his last visit there. Then the two families had all been on the terrace overhanging a sea so calm and clear that every star was reflected in the waters. Williams had cried "Buona notte!" and Trelawny had rowed himself on board the *Bolivar* at anchor in the bay. From afar he had listened to Jane singing some merry tune to the accompaniment of her guitar. Shelley's shrill laugh had pierced the quiet night, and Trelawny had looked back with regret on a set of human beings who had seemed to him the happiest and most united in the whole world.

His reverie was broken by a shriek from the nurse Caterina, as crossing the hall she saw him

in the doorway. He went upstairs and unan-
nounced entered the room where Mary and Jane
sat waiting. He could not speak a word. Mary
Shelley's hazel eyes fixed themselves on his with
a terrible intensity. She cried out: "Is there no
hope?" Trelawny, without answering, left the
room, and told the servant to take the children to
the two poor mothers.

CHAPTER XXXVII

LAST LINKS

MARY wished to have Shelley buried near their little boy in the Roman cemetery which he had thought so beautiful, but the sanitary laws forbade that bodies once buried in quicklime on the sands should be transferred elsewhere. Trelawny suggested, therefore, that the remains should be burned on the shore, according to the custom of the ancient Greeks. When the day was fixed for this ceremony, he sent word to Byron and Hunt, who wished to be present, and came himself on the *Bolivar*. The Tuscan authorities had provided a squad of soldiers armed with mattocks and spades.

The remains of Williams were dug out first. Standing round on the loose sand that scorched their feet, his friends watched the soldiers at work and waited with curiosity and horror the first appearance of the body. A black silk handkerchief was pulled out, then some shreds of linen, a boot with the bone of the leg and the foot in it, then a shapeless mass of bones and flesh. The limbs separated from the trunk on being touched. The soldiers performed their work with long-handled tongs, nippers, poles with iron hooks, spikes, and divers other tools all resembling implements of torture.

"Is that a human body?" exclaimed Byron. "Why, it's more like the carcase of a sheep!"

He was greatly moved, and tried to hide his emotion, which he thought maudlin and unmanly, under an air of indifference. When they were lifting the skull, "Stop a moment, let me see the jaw," he said. "I can recognize by the teeth anyone with whom I have talked. I always watch the mouth, it tells me what the eyes try to conceal."

A funeral pyre had been prepared, Trelawny applied the fire, and the materials being dry and resinous the pine-wood flamed furiously, and the heat drove the spectators back. The body and skull burning fiercely gave the flames a silvery and wavy look of indescribable brightness and purity. When the heat was a little diminished Byron and Hunt threw on to the fire frankincense, salt and wine.

"Come," said Byron suddenly, "let us try the strength of these waters that drowned our friends. . . . How far out do you think they were when their boat sank?"

Perhaps mingled with his grief was the thought that he, who had swum the Hellespont, would not have let himself be drowned in this less dangerous sea.

He stripped, went into the water, and swam out. Trelawny and Hunt followed him. When they turned to look back at the pyre it seemed a mere little glittering patch upon the sand.

.   .   .   .

The ceremony was repeated next day for Shelley, who had been buried in the sand, nearer to Via Reggio, between the sea and a pine-wood.

The weather was glorious. In the strong sunlight, the yellow sands and the deep violet sea made a wonderful contrast. Above the trees, the snow-capped Apennines paved the sky with a cloudy and marmoreal background such as Shelley would have loved. All the children of the country-side were gathered round to witness so unusual a spectacle, but not a word was spoken among them. Byron himself was silent and thoughtful. "Ah, Will of iron! This, then, is all that remains of your splendid courage. . . . Like Prometheus you defied Jupiter, and behold . . ."

The soldiers dug for nearly an hour without finding the exact place. Suddenly a dull hollow sound following the blow of a mattock warned them that the iron had struck a skull. Byron shuddered. He thought of Shelley during the storm on Lake Leman, whose crossed arms, heroic yet impotent, had seemed to him at the time an accurate symbol of his life. "How brutally mistaken men have been about him! He was without exception the *best* and least selfish man I ever knew. And as perfect a gentleman as ever crossed a drawing-room."

The body had been covered with lime, which had almost completely carbonized it. Once more incense, oil and salt were thrown upon the flames, and more wine was poured over Shelley's dead body than he had ever consumed during life. The intense heat made the atmosphere tremulous and wavy. At the end of three hours the heart, which was unusually big, remained unconsumed. Trelawny snatched it from the fiery furnace, burning his hand severely in doing so. The frontal bone of the skull where it had been struck by the mattock fell off, and the brains literally seethed, bubbled and boiled as in a cauldron for a very long time.

Byron could not face this scene. As on the

previous day he stripped and swam to the *Bolivar,* which was anchored in the bay. Trelawny gathered together the fragments of bone and human ashes, and placed them in an oaken casket lined with black velvet, which he had brought with him.

The village children, looking on with all their eyes, told each other, that from these bones, once they reached England, the dead man would come to life.

．　　．　　．　　．　　．　　．　　．

Now to tell what became of the other actors in this story.

Sir Timothy Shelley lived to the age of ninety-one, dying in 1844. He made Mary a small allowance, but she had to promise not to publish her husband's posthumous poems, nor any biography of him so long as the old baronet lived. At his death, Percy Florence came into the title and the fortune, Harriet's son Charles having died in his eleventh year.

A common misfortune had united the two widows, Mary and Jane. For a long time they lived together in Italy, and afterwards in London. Shelley's friends were so faithful to them that Trelawny asked the hand of Mary in marriage, and a little later Hogg, the sceptic, asked the hand of Jane. Mary refused, saying that she thought Mary Shelley so pretty a name she wished to have it on her tombstone. Jane accepted, but then had to confess she had never been married to Williams. She still had a husband somewhere in India. This did not trouble Hogg, and freed them both from any ceremony. They never left each other, and lived under decorous appearances. Although Hogg was accurate and a hard worker, he was considered mediocre at the Bar, where he pleaded without warmth or eloquence. Towards the end of his life he became a timorous, disillusioned old gentleman, reading Greek and Latin all day long to kill time and cheat his immense boredom.

Claire remained on the Continent; was a governess in Russia, and at the death of Sir Timothy inherited the twelve thousand pounds left her by Shelley, and was freed from poverty.

The older they grew the more these three women quarrelled amongst themselves. Jane declared to every one that during the last months at Casa Magni Shelley had loved her alone. These assertions repeated to Mary exasperated her so much that she refused to see Jane again. Little by little Miranda became an old woman, a trifle deaf, but always charming. Her eyes would still sparkle when she spoke of the Poet.

During many years Claire occupied herself in writing a book in which she intended to point out, by the examples of Shelley, Byron and herself, how necessary it is to have only conventional ideas on the question of love. But, having had a mental illness, she was obliged to give up work during a long period. She passed the end of her life in Florence, where she became a Roman Catholic and occupied herself in charities.

One day in the spring of 1878 a young man searching for documents on Byron and Shelley came to ask her for reminiscences of them. When he pronounced these two names, there appeared beneath the old lady's wrinkles one of those smiles, girlish yet full of promises, which had made her so fascinating at eighteen.

"Come," she said, "I suppose you are as crass as most men, and think that I loved Byron?"

Then, as he looked at her with surprise:

"My young friend," said she, "no doubt you will know a woman's heart better some day. I was dazzled, but that does not mean love. It might perhaps have grown into love, but it never did."

There was a silence. The visitor, hesitating a little, asked:

ARIEL

"Have you never loved, Madame?"

A delicate blush suffused the withered cheeks, and this time she made no reply, gazing on the ground.

"Shelley?" he murmured.

"With all my heart and soul," she replied, without raising her eyes.

Then with a charming coquetry she gave him a tap on the cheek with her closed fan.

(1)

THE END